The History of Washington

CRAFTED BY SKRIUWER

Copyright © 2025 by Skriuwer.

All rights reserved. No part of this book may be used or reproduced in any form whatsoever without written permission except in the case of brief quotations in critical articles or reviews.

At **Skriuwer**, we're more than just a team—we're a global community of people who love books. In Frisian, "Skriuwer" means "writer," and that's at the heart of what we do: creating and sharing books with readers worldwide. Wherever you are in the world, **Skriuwer** is here to inspire learning.

Frisian is one of the oldest languages in Europe, closely related to English and Dutch, and is spoken by about **500,000 people** in the province of **Friesland** (Fryslân), located in the northern Netherlands. It's the second official language of the Netherlands, but like many minority languages, Frisian faces the challenge of survival in a modern, globalized world.

We're using the money we earn to promote the Frisian language.

For more information, contact : **kontakt@skriuwer.com** (www.skriuwer.com)

Disclaimer:
The images in this book are creative reinterpretations of historical scenes. While every effort was made to accurately capture the essence of the periods depicted, some illustrations may include artistic embellishments or approximations. They are intended to evoke the atmosphere and spirit of the times rather than serve as precise historical records.

TABLE OF CONTENTS

CHAPTER 1: BEFORE PEOPLE ARRIVED – THE LAND AND ITS ANCIENT PAST

- Geological forces shaping Washington
- Volcanoes, glaciers, and floods transforming the region
- Ancient wildlife and shifting climates

CHAPTER 2: EARLY NATIVE PEOPLES – CULTURES AND TRADITIONS

- Arrival and settlement by diverse tribes
- Hunting, fishing, and gathering practices
- Spiritual beliefs and social structures

CHAPTER 3: FIRST EUROPEAN GLIMPSES – EXPLORERS ON THE COAST

- Spanish, British, and other voyages mapping the shoreline
- Encounters with coastal tribes
- Claims and competition among European powers

CHAPTER 4: THE FUR TRADE ERA – COMPANIES AND TRAPPERS

- Hudson's Bay Company and rival traders
- Impact on Native Peoples and animal populations
- Formation of early trading posts

CHAPTER 5: MISSIONS AND EARLY SETTLERS – SPREADING BELIEFS AND BUILDING HOMES

- Missionary arrivals and goals
- Homesteads and frontier life challenges
- Tensions between settlers and Native communities

CHAPTER 6: CONFLICT AND CHANGE – TENSIONS BETWEEN NATIVE TRIBES AND NEWCOMERS

- *Cayuse War, Whitman Mission incident, and other clashes*
- *Broken treaties and misunderstandings*
- *Lasting impact on tribal lands and sovereignty*

CHAPTER 7: THE OREGON TRAIL AND WESTWARD MOVEMENT – SETTLERS FLOOD INTO THE REGION

- *Wagon train journeys and hardships*
- *Growth of farming and new towns*
- *Shifting balance with Native Tribes*

CHAPTER 8: WASHINGTON BECOMES A TERRITORY – LAW AND ORDER ON THE FRONTIER

- *Separation from Oregon Territory*
- *Governor Isaac Stevens and treaty-making*
- *Establishing territorial government institutions*

CHAPTER 9: GROWING TOWNS AND NEW INDUSTRIES – LOGGING, FISHING, AND FARMING

- *Expansion of sawmills and canneries*
- *Rise of agricultural communities*
- *Everyday life in emerging towns*

CHAPTER 10: RAILROADS AND ROADS – CONNECTING PEOPLE AND GOODS

- *Northern Pacific, Great Northern, and other lines*
- *Bridging remote areas and boosting trade*
- *Early road development and stagecoach routes*

CHAPTER 11: THE MAKING OF A STATE – WASHINGTON JOINS THE UNION

- Campaigns and steps toward statehood in 1889
- First constitution and official governance
- Political shifts and organizational milestones

CHAPTER 12: DAILY LIFE IN EARLY WASHINGTON – FAMILIES, SCHOOLS, AND TOWNS

- Family structures on homesteads and in small cities
- One-room schoolhouses and local traditions
- Social gatherings, dances, and community bonds

CHAPTER 13: NATIVE RESISTANCE AND TREATIES – BATTLES AND AGREEMENTS

- Major conflicts like the Yakama War and Puget Sound War
- Key treaties and their broken promises
- Shaping future legal struggles for tribal rights

CHAPTER 14: BOOM AND BUST – ECONOMIC HIGHS AND LOWS

- Real estate speculation and mining rushes
- Coal, timber, and agricultural cycles
- Vulnerability of single-resource economies

CHAPTER 15: EARLY MINING ADVENTURES – SEARCHING FOR GOLD AND OTHER TREASURES

- Panning, sluicing, and hard rock mining techniques
- Formation and collapse of mining camps
- Influence on local businesses and transportation

CHAPTER 16: CULTURAL GROWTH – CHURCHES, NEWSPAPERS, AND COMMUNITY ACTIVITIES

- *Spread of different denominations and congregations*
- *Role of local journalism and printed news*
- *Social clubs, charity events, and evolving civic life*

CHAPTER 17: EARLY 1900S CHANGES – LABOR MOVEMENTS AND SOCIAL SHIFTS

- *Strikes and union organizing in mills and shipyards*
- *Emergence of women's suffrage and prohibition efforts*
- *Progressive-era politics shaping public reforms*

CHAPTER 18: FAMOUS FIGURES – LEADERS, VISIONARIES, AND LOCAL HEROES

- *Influential governors, entrepreneurs, and activists*
- *Unsung everyday heroes in medicine, teaching, and tribal leadership*
- *Lasting impacts on Washington's identity*

CHAPTER 19: REGIONAL DIFFERENCES – EASTERN AND WESTERN WASHINGTON

- *Cascade Range as a cultural and economic boundary*
- *Wet coastal forests vs. dry farmland and orchards*
- *Bridging the divide through trade, transportation, and cooperation*

CHAPTER 20: LAST REFLECTIONS ON EARLY WASHINGTON – LESSONS AND LEGACIES

- *Reviewing main themes of conflict, unity, and growth*
- *Cultural resilience, environmental challenges, and cooperation*
- *Enduring influence on modern Washington's character*

CHAPTER 1

Before People Arrived – The Land and Its Ancient Past

Washington, as we know it today, is a beautiful place with tall mountains, thick forests, and rushing rivers. But there was a time long ago, before any people lived here, when the land looked very different. In this chapter, we will explore how the land of Washington formed. We will talk about volcanoes, glaciers, and the slow work of nature over many thousands of years. This will help us understand why Washington looks the way it does. This story begins millions of years before humans arrived.

Ancient Land Shapes

The shape of Washington's land began a very long time ago. The continents themselves have been slowly drifting for hundreds of millions of years. Scientists call this movement "continental drift." Over these long periods, landmasses have collided, separated, and changed shape. Washington is located in a region known for its tectonic plates. One of the biggest plates here is the Juan de Fuca Plate, which moves and pushes under the North American Plate. This movement is why there are volcanoes along the Cascade Range.

Imagine looking at Washington when it was underwater, since large parts of it were once covered by the ocean. Over millions of years, the ocean waters rose and fell. Layers of rock formed at the bottom of the sea. Sometimes, earthquakes forced these layers above the surface. So, pieces of ocean floor became mountains and hills. These changes happened so slowly that you would never notice them if you were living during those times. But over millions of years, these small movements built the shape of Washington.

The Power of Volcanoes

Volcanoes have played a large role in shaping Washington's land. The Cascade Range is a group of volcanoes that stretches from Northern California to British Columbia in Canada. Some of the famous volcanoes in Washington include Mount Rainier, Mount St. Helens, Mount Adams, and Mount Baker. These volcanoes formed because the Juan de Fuca Plate slides underneath the North American Plate. When this happens, the rocks deep underground melt and rise up as magma. If the magma breaks through the ground, it erupts as lava and ash, building the cone shape of a volcano.

Over thousands of years, these volcanoes erupted many times. Each eruption left layers of ash, rock, and other materials. This changed the land around them. After an eruption, the volcano might be taller or sometimes lower if part of it collapsed. These changes also affect rivers and streams because large mudflows can flow down the mountainsides. They carry rocks and debris, making new valleys or filling old ones. When we look at Washington's volcanoes today, we can still see signs of past eruptions in the rock layers.

Glaciers and Ice Ages

One of the most important forces that shaped Washington's landscape was the Ice Age. During the Ice Age, huge sheets of ice called glaciers covered much of North America. In Washington, large glaciers formed on the mountains and in the valleys. These glaciers moved slowly, like giant rivers of ice. As they moved, they scraped the ground, carved out valleys, and left behind mounds of rocks. This is why some parts of Washington have large, smooth valleys while others have ridges or gravel hills.

Think of a glacier like a bulldozer. As it slides across the land, it pushes soil and rocks ahead of it, forming piles called moraines. It also grinds the rocks beneath it, shaping them into new forms. When the climate got warmer, the ice melted, leaving behind lakes and new paths for rivers. This is how some of Washington's river valleys were created. Even today, you can see the remains of glaciers in the high mountains. They are much smaller than they used to be, but they remind us of the powerful ice that once covered so much land.

Ancient Lakes and Dry Regions

Because of the glaciers, Washington once had huge lakes. When ice dams formed, they blocked rivers, creating large bodies of water behind them. One famous example is Glacial Lake Missoula, which was actually in Montana but affected areas to the west, including parts of Washington. When the ice dam that held back Lake Missoula broke, an enormous flood swept across eastern Washington. This is called the Missoula Flood. It happened many times, shaping the landscape in a dramatic way. These floods dug deep channels and canyons, leaving rocky features and dry waterfalls behind.

If you visit eastern Washington today, you might see large canyons that look like dried-up riverbeds. Places like the Grand Coulee and Dry Falls are examples of the power of these floods. People sometimes call them "channeled scablands" because they look so rough and scarred. These floods were not small. They were some of the biggest floods known on Earth. They changed the land forever, leaving behind a unique landscape that we can still see.

Development of the Cascade and Olympic Mountains

On the western side of Washington are the Olympic Mountains. These mountains are different from the Cascades because they did not form from volcanoes. Instead, they formed from older ocean rocks that were pushed upwards. The Olympics are very wet, with many rainy days each year, which helps create thick forests of fir, hemlock, and cedar. The moisture comes from the Pacific Ocean, which lies just to the west of the Olympic Peninsula.

The Cascade Range, running north to south, splits Washington into two distinct regions. West of the Cascades is wetter and has dense forests. East of the Cascades is drier and can have rolling hills, wide plains, or farmland. This division has always been important, even in ancient times, because it affects where animals live and how plants grow.

Wildlife Before People

Before humans appeared, Washington was home to many kinds of animals, some of which are no longer here. Mastodons and mammoths once roamed. These were large elephant-like creatures with big tusks. There were also giant sloths, which were bigger than bears. Saber-toothed cats, with their long sharp teeth, lived in parts of North America, possibly including the Pacific Northwest.

Plant life was also different, with large stretches of conifer forests. In wetter regions, ferns and mosses grew thick on the forest floor. In the drier east, grasslands spread out, making homes for different kinds of animals. The climate changed over time, and so did the kinds of creatures that could survive here.

Shifting Climates and Landforms

The climate in Washington changed many times over millions of years. Sometimes it was colder, bringing more ice and glaciers. Other times it was warmer, melting ice and letting forests spread. Each shift changed the habitats of animals and the growth of plants. Rivers changed course and new valleys formed. Volcanoes erupted and shaped new land. This never-ending process created the land that the first people would eventually find when they arrived.

Even after people came, the land kept changing. Eruptions, floods, and earthquakes did not stop. But for many thousands of years, these natural events were the main forces shaping Washington. There were no cities or roads to change the environment. There were only forests, rivers, plains, and wildlife.

Looking Ahead

In this chapter, we learned about the ancient past of Washington. We saw how tectonic plates, volcanoes, glaciers, and floods shaped the region. We also got a glimpse of the ancient animals and plants that lived here. This sets the stage for understanding how the people who would eventually arrive had to adapt to a land of towering mountains, big rivers, and deep forests.

In the next chapter, we will learn about the earliest Native Peoples who made Washington their home. We will see how they used the resources of the land—fish, game, and plants—to build societies that lasted thousands of years. Understanding the land is important to understanding the people. The story of Washington truly begins when the first people arrived.

CHAPTER 2

Early Native Peoples – Cultures and Traditions

Thousands of years ago, people traveled to North America from Asia, crossing a land bridge that once connected the continents. Over time, some groups moved into the Pacific Northwest region we now call Washington. They found a land rich in resources, with rivers full of salmon, forests with deer and elk, and shorelines with clams and other seafood. They also found large cedar trees, which they learned to shape into canoes, houses, and tools.

In this chapter, we will explore the early Native Peoples of Washington. We will look at how they lived, what they ate, and how their cultures were shaped by the land. We will also see how they respected nature and built lasting traditions that remain important to many tribes today.

The Arrival of the First People

We do not know exactly when the first people arrived in Washington, but some scientists believe it may have been more than 10,000 years ago. These early people were hunters and gatherers. They followed the animals they hunted, like mammoths, bison, and other large game. They also fished in the rivers and collected plants and roots. Over time, the climate changed, and the kinds of animals that lived here changed too. Large Ice Age animals like mammoths disappeared, so people hunted deer, elk, and smaller creatures.

These first people did not have written records. Instead, they passed down knowledge through stories, songs, and oral traditions. Each tribe had its own way of understanding the world around them. Some believed in a Great Spirit or many spirits that lived in nature, such as spirits of the sky, rivers, and animals. This respect for nature shaped how they hunted, gathered, and fished, so they would not deplete the land's resources.

Growth of Distinct Tribes

As time went on, different groups in Washington developed their own languages, customs, and ways of life. Tribes settled along rivers, on the coast, or in forested areas. Some groups moved seasonally, going to higher elevations in the summer to hunt and gather berries, then returning to lower river valleys in the winter. Each region offered different resources.

1. **Coastal Tribes**: Tribes like the Makah, Quinault, and Quileute lived along the ocean. They relied heavily on fishing and whaling. They carved large canoes from cedar trees. These canoes could hold many people and travel far across the ocean to hunt whales. Coastal tribes built plank houses from cedar planks. These houses could shelter large families and store dried fish, roots, and berries for winter. Coastal life was tied to the tides, the wind, and the sea's abundance.

2. **Puget Sound Tribes**: Tribes like the Duwamish, Suquamish, and others lived in the area around the Puget Sound. They also relied on fishing, using skillfully made nets and weirs to catch salmon during spawning seasons. They gathered shellfish along the shores. Cedar trees were just as important for building homes and crafting clothes. Many ceremonies centered on the salmon runs, because salmon were a vital food source.

3. **River Tribes in the Interior**: Farther inland, along rivers like the Columbia, Yakima, and Snake, tribes like the Yakama, Umatilla, and others hunted game on the plains and fished the rivers. They traveled to harvest roots like the camas bulb, an important source of nutrition. During salmon runs, people gathered at traditional fishing spots. One well-known fishing area was Celilo Falls on the Columbia River. Tribes would meet there not just to fish, but also to trade goods and share news.

4. **Plateau and Mountain Tribes**: Tribes like the Spokane, Colville, and Flathead lived in the plateau regions and near mountain ranges. They made use of pine forests, open meadows, and rivers. They fished, hunted deer and elk, and collected wild plants. They also traveled with the seasons, following game and harvest times. They built shelters like mat lodges covered with grasses or bark. These were different from the cedar plank houses along the coast.

Culture and Spiritual Beliefs

Despite their differences, many tribes shared a deep respect for the natural world. They believed that animals, trees, rivers, and even rocks had spirits or life force. This outlook taught them to use resources wisely. If they hunted a deer, they used nearly every part of it for food, clothing, and tools. They gave thanks to the animal's spirit. They also held ceremonies to honor the salmon returning to the rivers or the first berries ripening in the summer.

Storytelling was a key part of passing on history and lessons. Elders told stories around the fire about how the world was created or how certain landmarks came to be. These stories taught children about tribal rules, moral lessons, and survival skills. Songs and dances were also important, often performed at potlatches or special gatherings. Potlatches were ceremonies where a host would give away gifts to guests, showing generosity and respect.

Daily Life: Food, Clothing, and Shelter

Food: Salmon was a main food for many tribes in Washington, especially those near rivers and coasts. They dried or smoked salmon to store for winter. They also gathered berries like huckleberries, blackberries, and salal berries. In the eastern regions, tribes would harvest root crops like camas bulbs, which they cooked in pit ovens. Hunting was crucial, especially for deer and elk. Tribes that lived near the ocean ate clams, mussels, crabs, and even seals or whales if they had the skill to hunt them.

Clothing: Clothing depended on the resources nearby. Coastal tribes often used woven cedar bark to make capes, skirts, and hats, as cedar bark can be softened and woven like fabric. They also used animal skins. Inland tribes used deer and elk hides, which they tanned and sewed into dresses, leggings, and moccasins. Decorations like beads, shells, and feathers were common.

Shelter: Coastal tribes built large cedar plank houses. These were sturdy structures with thick walls of split cedar planks. A single house could hold many families. In the interior, many tribes built conical or round lodges covered with mats or bark. Some used semi-subterranean homes, partly dug into the ground, for warmth during cold winters.

Trade and Communication

Tribes in Washington were not isolated. They traded goods and communicated with tribes far away. They used canoes to travel along rivers and across bodies of water. Trading centers sprang up where people from different areas met to exchange items. Coastal tribes might trade dried fish, shells, and cedar goods for buffalo hides or obsidian from the interior tribes. Obsidian was used to make sharp tools and arrowheads.

Some tribes became known as skilled traders or craftspeople. They learned to speak bits of other tribes' languages or created trade languages like Chinook Jargon. This helped them barter and form alliances. Trade also spread ideas, art styles, and spiritual practices. This network allowed tribes to keep in contact and help each other in times of need.

Art and Craftsmanship

Wood carving was a big part of coastal culture. They carved canoes from single cedar trunks, which sometimes were huge. They also carved masks, totem poles, and house posts. Each design had meaning, often telling the story of a family or representing an important spirit. Weaving was another important art. Women wove baskets from cedar bark and local grasses. These baskets could be watertight, used for cooking or storing liquids.

In the interior, beads and porcupine quills were used to decorate clothing and bags. After horses arrived in North America (brought by Europeans), some tribes adopted horse culture, but that happened later. In early times, travel was mostly on foot or by canoe. Still, the craftsmanship in toolmaking, weaving, and shelter-building was remarkable.

Social Structures and Leadership

Tribal groups were often made up of extended families. Leaders or chiefs emerged based on wisdom, hunting skill, or spiritual power. Some tribes also had councils of elders who made decisions for the group. These leaders had to be good at building agreement and keeping peace. Conflicts did happen, sometimes leading to raids or battles over resources. But many tribes preferred trade and alliances to support each other, especially in harsh winters or during times of scarcity.

Marriage often linked different families or even different tribes. Ceremonies could be simple or elaborate, depending on the tribe. Gifts, feasts, and dances might mark a wedding event. The bond between families helped maintain peace and created networks of support.

Respect for Nature and the Spiritual World

The tribes of Washington had a worldview that made nature and spirit connected. This included the idea that every part of the environment had a purpose. If a tribe relied too much on one resource, they might lose respect for the balance of nature. Stories taught children not to waste or harm animals unnecessarily. Elders reminded everyone that nature was a gift that sustained life.

Spiritual leaders, sometimes called shamans, played an important role. They sought guidance from the spirit world, healed the sick, and interpreted dreams or omens. Rituals and ceremonies were ways to keep harmony with the spirits. People believed that if they cared for the land and treated animals with respect, the spirits would keep providing for them.

The First Signs of Change

For many centuries, life for the tribes of Washington continued with little outside influence. They traded with each other, built families, and practiced their cultural traditions. Yet, change was on the horizon. By the 1700s, European explorers would begin sailing along the coast. At first, tribes might have only heard rumors of these newcomers from other tribes. Over time, the newcomers would land, bringing new goods like metal tools and new diseases that the Native Peoples had never known.

But in this chapter, we remain in the time before any major outside contact. We see how the people of Washington lived off the land and developed strong cultures. They built homes, told stories, held potlatches, and cared for each other. This was their world, filled with cedar trees, salmon, deer, and the deep sense that all life was interconnected.

Looking Ahead

The early Native Peoples of Washington set the foundation for what was to come. They survived in this land for thousands of years. They learned its rhythms and respected its power. When Europeans arrived, everything changed in ways that Native Peoples could not have imagined. This contact brought trade, but it also brought conflict and disease.

In the next chapters, we will see how explorers and traders arrived, how missions were formed, and how settlers and Native Tribes sometimes clashed. But we will also see how the Native Peoples held on to their culture and traditions, even as outside pressures grew. Understanding these early chapters helps us respect the resilience and wisdom of the first Washingtonians.

CHAPTER 3

First European Glimpses – Explorers on the Coast

During the late 1700s, explorers from Europe began sailing along the coastline of what is now Washington. They were searching for new lands, trade routes, and wealth. At first, they did not know much about the people who lived there or the geography of the region. Over time, Spanish, British, and other explorers slowly made detailed notes about the bays, islands, rivers, and weather patterns. These early voyages opened the door for more contact with Native Tribes. They also set the stage for disputes between different European powers about who had the right to claim this land.

In this chapter, we will learn how these explorers arrived, what they saw, and how they dealt with the local tribes. We will also learn about some of the major figures who put Washington on the European maps. These glimpses were not always peaceful or fair. Still, they were the first steps toward big changes that would soon follow.

Setting the Stage

By the 1700s, European nations such as Spain and Great Britain had established colonies in many parts of the Americas. Spain had colonies in Mexico and along the California coast. Britain had colonies along the Atlantic coast and in parts of Canada. Russia also had outposts in Alaska. France had colonies in parts of Canada, though they eventually lost control of much of their territory after conflicts with the British. The Pacific Northwest, stretching from California's northern border all the way up to Alaska, remained mostly unexplored by Europeans. Yet rumors and old stories hinted that there might be a sailing route through this area to the Atlantic, called the Northwest Passage.

The search for the Northwest Passage attracted many explorers. They hoped to find a shortcut to link the Atlantic and Pacific Oceans. Such a route would make trading with Asia faster and more profitable. Although the Spanish had a strong claim to the west coast of the Americas, the British and others wanted to push north in hopes of finding new trade opportunities. As a result, ships began sailing into the waters off what is now Washington, scouting bays and looking for rivers that might lead to a passage across the continent.

Early Spanish Explorations

Spain was one of the first European powers to send ships north from Mexico to explore the Pacific Coast. They wanted to keep other nations away and defend their rights to the land. However, the Spanish discovered that the coastline in this region could be dangerous. Fog, rocky shores, and storms made sailing risky. Moreover, they had limited supplies and ships.

One early Spanish expedition was led by Bruno de Heceta and Juan Francisco de la Bodega y Quadra in 1775. Their ships sailed up the coast, noting various points along the way. Heceta and Bodega y Quadra made an effort to chart the coastline carefully. They spotted what they believed to be a large bay with strong currents, which might have been the mouth of the Columbia River. Because of poor weather and some sickness aboard their ships, they were not able to explore the river closely. Still, they kept records of its possible location.

A few years later, Spanish expeditions continued sailing to the Pacific Northwest. They built small outposts in places like Nootka

Sound on Vancouver Island (now part of Canada) to strengthen their claim. Though not exactly in modern Washington, Nootka Sound was an important hub for Spanish activity in the region. From there, Spanish ships would sometimes sail south and explore the coastline, trading with local tribes and making maps. These expeditions did not immediately lead to large settlements in Washington, but they did help Spain to claim the area on paper.

The British Appear

While Spain was exploring from the south, Great Britain began sending expeditions from the north or across the Pacific. One famous British explorer was Captain James Cook, who sailed into the Pacific Northwest in 1778. Though Captain Cook is more famously linked with Hawaii and other Pacific islands, he also went up the coast. He was searching for the Northwest Passage and looking for new resources. Cook did not spend much time in what is now Washington, but his journey sparked British interest in the region's fur-bearing animals, especially sea otters. News spread that sea otter pelts from the Northwest Coast could fetch very high prices in China. This would become more significant in the next chapter, which covers the fur trade era.

After Cook, other British explorers arrived. Among them was Captain George Vancouver, who made a more detailed survey in the early 1790s. Vancouver was tasked with mapping the northwest coastline and gathering information. In April 1792, he sailed into what is now the Strait of Juan de Fuca, located between the Olympic Peninsula and Vancouver Island. This strait is a key entrance to Puget Sound. Vancouver's ships sailed into Puget Sound and began exploring its inlets and bays. He and his crew took careful notes, naming many places along the way. Some of these names remain today, such as Puget Sound (named after Lieutenant Peter Puget).

Vancouver's explorations were quite extensive. He took smaller boats into narrow channels, noting the shape of the coastline. He met with local tribes who sometimes traded fish and other items. Vancouver's crew described the tall cedar forests, the mountainous terrain, and the cloudy skies. They realized that the region was full of natural resources, especially timber and fish. Vancouver was certain that the area had potential for future settlement or trading posts. His detailed maps and journals gave Europeans a clearer picture of what was there.

Encounters with Native Tribes

When European explorers arrived, they usually came by ship, anchoring off the coast or sailing into bays. Some tribes were curious and paddled out in canoes to see these strange vessels. Others were cautious and waited on shore. Different tribes responded in different ways. Some welcomed trade, offering fish, animal skins, or woven baskets in exchange for metal tools, beads, and other goods. Others avoided the newcomers, worried about possible danger.

Communication was difficult because the tribes spoke many different languages. Some explorers tried to learn a few words or used gestures to get their meaning across. In some cases, misunderstandings led to small conflicts. However, many first meetings were peaceful. The explorers usually wanted fresh water, food, or a safe place to anchor. The tribes often wanted metal items, blankets, or trinkets. These early encounters did not involve large-scale fighting or settlement, because the explorers were not yet building permanent homes. They were mostly charting the land or looking for the Northwest Passage.

Still, these brief contacts were not without problems. In some places, diseases like smallpox had already started to spread from earlier contacts with Europeans to the south or from trade networks that brought infected people or objects north. Tribes had no immunity to these diseases, leading to many deaths. Explorers sometimes did not realize they were carrying illnesses with them. Even if they had no ill intent, their arrival could have devastating effects on local populations.

French and Russian Interests

While Spain and Great Britain took the lead, other nations also had an interest in the Pacific Northwest. France, which once controlled parts of Canada, had lost much territory. Yet some French traders and explorers still ventured into the region, hoping to find furs or new routes. They did not have the same government support that Spain or Britain did, so their explorations were smaller in scale.

Russia had a more direct claim in Alaska, where Russian traders hunted sea otters and other fur-bearing animals. Some Russian ships sailed farther south in search of new hunting grounds. They met with local Native Peoples, sometimes establishing temporary camps. However, the Russians never built large outposts in what is now Washington. Their focus stayed mostly on Alaska and parts of what is now Canada.

The Nootka Crisis and International Tensions

One important event in the late 1700s was the Nootka Crisis between Spain and Great Britain. Although Nootka Sound is in Canada, it affected the entire region. The crisis began when the Spanish navy seized British ships in Nootka Sound. The Spanish claimed that the entire Pacific Northwest was their territory, based on earlier discoveries. The British argued that Spain had not truly settled or occupied most of the coastline, so Britain had the right to trade there as well.

Tensions rose, and for a time it looked like war might break out between Spain and Britain over distant lands on the Northwest Coast. Eventually, they signed agreements known as the Nootka Conventions, which allowed both nations to trade and explore the region. While this did not directly say who would own the land that would become Washington, it effectively ended Spain's sole claim. Over time, Spanish influence in the Pacific Northwest began to wane, and Britain took a leading role.

The Columbia River Discovery

Another key moment was the discovery of the mouth of the Columbia River by an American captain named Robert Gray in 1792. While not British or Spanish, this American arrival also shaped the future of Washington. Captain Gray sailed in a ship called the Columbia Rediviva. He had already been trading in the area for sea otter pelts. During his voyage, Gray noticed a large estuary with strong currents, which he suspected to be a major river.

Sailing into the mouth of the river, he claimed it for the United States, naming it the Columbia after his ship. This claim would later become important when the United States argued that Washington and Oregon belonged to them. Though the Spanish and British had passed by the mouth of the Columbia before, none had sailed into it the way Gray did. This event marked a significant point in territorial claims, because now three major powers—Spain, Britain, and the United States—had reasons to say they owned parts of the Pacific Northwest.

Captain Vancouver arrived shortly after Gray. At first, Vancouver had doubts that there was a large river because he had not seen a major entrance. But when he learned of Gray's discovery, he sent a small boat to explore. This boat confirmed the river's size, though the British continued to think they had rights to the land. Over time, the matter of who owned the Columbia River region would become a heated issue.

Impact of Early Exploration on Native Peoples

From the perspective of many tribes in the region, these new visitors were just passing through. Some tribes saw new opportunities to trade. Metal knives and axes were far superior to stone tools. Cloth, beads, and other items were interesting and useful. However, this contact was also dangerous. Diseases such as smallpox or measles sometimes spread to tribes that had never experienced them. Even a brief encounter could lead to an outbreak, especially if the tribes had no natural resistance.

Moreover, tribes began to sense that these visitors were not just explorers. The way the Europeans claimed land for distant kings or governments was strange to the Native Peoples. The idea that land could belong to someone far away made little sense to tribes who had shared the land for centuries. This difference in understanding set the stage for future conflicts.

Still, at the time of these early voyages, large-scale settlement by Europeans had not yet begun. Most Native tribes went on with their daily lives, fishing, hunting, and trading with each other as they had for generations. They might see a foreign ship one month, then not see another for a long time. Only when the fur trade and missionary activities began to grow did tribes realize that changes were coming faster than they expected.

Scientific Interest and Mapping

Some explorers were not just looking for gold or a passage to the Atlantic. They were also curious about plants, animals, and geography. Naturalists sometimes accompanied voyages, collecting specimens of unknown species. They drew sketches of the local wildlife, wrote notes on the climate, and studied the geology of the region. These scientific observations helped Europeans understand the richness of the Pacific Northwest. They learned about cedar trees, salmon runs, bald eagles, and other species.

During their voyages, these explorers created maps that were more accurate than ever before. They named bays, channels, and islands. This made it easier for future ships to navigate. These maps also proved to European powers that the region had valuable harbors and might be suitable for settlement or resource extraction. Once the region had been mapped, more ships ventured in, and eventually traders and settlers followed.

A Mix of Curiosity and Competition

The tone of these early explorations was a mix of curiosity and competition. Explorers were excited to discover new landforms and meet new people. But they also carried the ambition of their home nations. They claimed land, named places, and wrote about the potential for wealth. Each expedition tried to gain an advantage over the others.

- **Spain** wanted to preserve its claim over the entire west coast of the Americas, going back to the 1500s.
- **Great Britain** sought to expand its global power and find new trade routes and resources.
- **The United States** was a new nation growing quickly, looking for places to trade and settle.
- **Russia** also hoped to keep extending its fur operations in Alaska and possibly farther south.

This race for influence did not yet involve large armies or direct wars in Washington, but tensions hovered in the background. If an explorer found a valuable area, it might attract the attention of his nation, which could then send more ships or traders.

Encounters with the Land Itself

Beyond dealing with local tribes or other European ships, explorers also struggled with the land and weather. The Pacific Northwest can be rainy and foggy for much of the year. Thick fog often appeared, making navigation dangerous. The rocky coastline was full of hidden reefs and narrow passages. Storms could blow ships off course, leaving them lost at sea. Fresh water was sometimes hard to find along the rocky shores, forcing ships to ration water carefully.

In some cases, explorers had to stay anchored for weeks in a sheltered bay, waiting for better weather. During these stays, they explored on foot, gathering firewood, fishing, and making repairs to their ships. They might also meet local people who showed them where to find streams or taught them how to prepare certain local foods. For the explorers, these interactions could mean survival.

Seeds of Settlement

Although the explorers did not establish large towns right away, their journals and maps planted the seeds of future settlement. Back in Europe or along the East Coast of the United States, governments and merchants read about this lush land filled with fish and timber. They also learned about the potential wealth from the fur trade. Little by little, the idea grew that people could move there, build forts or trading posts, and make profit.

For Native Peoples, the future would become more complicated. These foreign ships would soon be followed by traders who wanted furs. Next would come missionaries who wanted to spread their faith. Finally, farmers and families looking for a new life would arrive. But at the end of the 1700s, this was still just beginning.

Looking Ahead

In this chapter, we saw how European explorers first glimpsed Washington from the coast. Spain and Britain were the major powers, with the United States starting to show interest. Each nation had different goals, but all of them wanted to claim or profit from the region. The local tribes had varying reactions, from curiosity to caution, and disease began to appear as an unwelcome companion to these foreign visits.

As we move into the next chapter, we will see how the fur trade grew in importance. The fur trade era brought new players into the Pacific Northwest, including powerful companies like the Hudson's Bay Company. Trappers and traders fanned out across the land, setting up posts and changing the way Native Peoples lived. This chapter closes the book on the first glimpses by European explorers. The next phase would be more about business, trapping, and the competition for profits from the vast natural resources of Washington.

CHAPTER 4

The Fur Trade Era – Companies and Trappers

With European explorers mapping the coastline and finding resources, the next stage of Washington's early history took shape: the fur trade. In this chapter, we will explore how companies and independent traders rushed to the region to hunt for valuable furs, especially sea otter and beaver pelts. This activity brought more direct contact with Native Peoples, altered local economies, and led to conflicts between rival companies. It also set the stage for future settlements and disputes over who controlled the land.

By the early 1800s, the fur trade in the Pacific Northwest was booming. We will see how major companies such as the Hudson's Bay Company from Britain and other ventures shaped this era. We will also learn about the hardships faced by trappers in the wilderness and how Native Tribes played a key role in helping or hindering the trade. Finally, we will look at how this trade eventually declined, giving way to other economic activities.

The Value of Furs

Furs, particularly sea otter and beaver, were highly prized in Europe and Asia during the 18th and early 19th centuries. Sea otter pelts were prized in China, where they could fetch extremely high prices. Beaver pelts were in demand in Europe for making hats and other clothing items. Because of this strong demand, traders saw an opportunity to make great profits if they could get furs from the Pacific Northwest.

When Captain Cook's crew returned to Europe from their voyage, they brought stories of how easily they had obtained sea otter pelts from Native Peoples along the coast. Rumors spread among merchants, and soon ships from Britain, the United States, and other countries began arriving to buy or trade for pelts. Some of these traders stayed close to the coast, sailing from bay to bay. Others journeyed inland, making deals with tribes along large rivers like the Columbia.

Maritime Fur Trade

At first, much of the fur trade was maritime-based. This means traders used ships to visit coastal villages, where they would exchange items like metal tools, guns, blankets, or beads for sea otter skins. They often traveled to places like Nootka Sound (on Vancouver Island) or around the Olympic Peninsula, anchoring in safe coves. The tribes living along these coasts were willing to trade furs they had collected from hunting sea otters. Some tribes saw this as an opportunity to gain items they had never seen before. Metal knives, pots, and other goods could make daily life easier.

However, there were challenges. Sea otters lived in kelp beds and rocky areas along the coast. Overhunting soon became a problem. When traders realized how valuable sea otter pelts were, they pushed the tribes to hunt more. They also hired hunters from other areas or even brought Aleut hunters from Alaska, who were skilled at sea otter hunting. The otter population began to drop, and it became harder to find enough animals to meet the high demand. This scarcity led traders to explore more of the coastline or move inland in search of other furs.

Moving Inland: The Columbia River and Beyond

As the sea otter population declined, traders turned to other fur-bearing animals, especially beaver. Beaver pelts were also valuable in Europe, used for making hats that were fashionable at the time. Traders discovered that the interior regions of the Pacific Northwest had plenty of rivers and streams where beavers lived. To reach these interior areas, traders began establishing posts along rivers. The Columbia River was a major route into the interior. It offered a way to travel by boat, although navigating its rapids and waterfalls was dangerous.

Soon, different groups of trappers spread out across the valleys and mountains of what is now Washington, Idaho, Oregon, and parts of British Columbia. Some traveled by canoe along rivers, while others rode horses through passes in the Cascade Range. They trapped beavers using steel traps, which were more effective than wooden or bone traps the Native Peoples had used in the past. Many Native Americans became trappers or guides themselves, working alongside the newcomers or trading with them.

Key Players: Hudson's Bay Company and Others

Hudson's Bay Company

One of the most influential organizations in the fur trade era was the British-owned Hudson's Bay Company (HBC). Founded in 1670, the HBC already had a strong presence in Canada's central and eastern regions. By the early 1800s, the company looked west to expand its reach. HBC believed in setting up strong, centrally managed trading posts. Trappers, both Native and European, could bring furs to these posts in exchange for supplies. Then the company would ship the furs to markets abroad.

In the Columbia District (a large area that included modern-day Washington), the HBC established Fort Vancouver (near present-day

Vancouver, Washington) in 1825. This post became the HBC's main headquarters in the region. From Fort Vancouver, they managed other smaller posts and coordinated trapping expeditions. The post itself became a small community, with farms, livestock, and workshops. It attracted French-Canadian trappers, British employees, and even some Hawaiian laborers brought in by the company. Native Americans also came to trade, and there were intermarriages between HBC employees and Native women.

Fort Vancouver played a central role in the region's economy. It stored large quantities of supplies such as blankets, metal goods, and food. Trappers returning from long expeditions in the mountains would bring their furs here. They would rest, trade furs for fresh supplies, and then head out again. This pattern continued year after year. The HBC also tried to maintain good relationships with local tribes, though tensions did arise at times.

North West Company

Before the Hudson's Bay Company took full control of the area, another British enterprise called the North West Company (NWC) was active. The NWC was based in Montreal, Canada, and it used a network of trappers and traders who traveled deep into the interior. The NWC established posts in areas that would later become eastern Washington. However, competition between the HBC and the NWC caused problems. Both companies wanted to control the fur trade, leading to fierce rivalry.

Eventually, the two companies merged in 1821, with the Hudson's Bay Company remaining as the main name. This merger gave the HBC a near monopoly over the fur trade in the Pacific Northwest, allowing it to manage resources and control prices more easily.

American Fur Interests

On the American side, John Jacob Astor, a wealthy businessman from New York, created the Pacific Fur Company. He established Fort Astoria (at the mouth of the Columbia River) in 1811. However, the

War of 1812 between the United States and Britain led to the sale of Fort Astoria to the North West Company. American influence in the region's fur trade waned for a time. But as we will see in later chapters, American settlers would eventually come in greater numbers, setting the stage for new power struggles.

Life as a Trapper

Life as a fur trapper in the Pacific Northwest was not easy. Men traveled for months in harsh conditions, carrying steel traps, rifles, and basic supplies. In winter, heavy snow could block passes and freeze rivers, making travel dangerous. In spring, melting snow could cause rivers to flood, washing away traps. Mountain lions, wolves, and bears also posed threats to trappers. If a trapper got injured far from a trading post, help might be impossible to find.

Despite these risks, the potential rewards were high. A single beaver pelt could earn a good amount of money, or be traded for supplies that were otherwise expensive. Many trappers came from rough backgrounds or were used to living off the land. They learned survival skills, how to make lean-to shelters, and how to track animals. Some were independent, while others worked directly for companies like the HBC. Company trappers sometimes worked in organized brigades, traveling together for safety and sharing the workload of hauling supplies and furs.

Native guides often played a crucial role. They showed trappers the best routes, warned them of dangerous conditions, and sometimes helped negotiate with local tribes. In return, they expected payment or goods, and some gained status as important figures in the fur trade. However, misunderstandings and unfair treatment could occur. Some trappers took advantage of Native guides, paying them poorly. Others built genuine partnerships and friendships that lasted many years.

Changing Native Economies

For many Native Tribes, the fur trade brought changes to their daily life. At first, it seemed like a good opportunity. Tribes could trade furs for metal tools, blankets, guns, or other goods that made hunting and fishing easier. Guns, in particular, changed the balance of power among some tribes. Tribes that gained access to guns could hunt more effectively or protect their lands against enemies.

Yet, the fur trade also caused problems. Over-harvesting of beavers and other animals disrupted ecosystems. Beaver dams were important for maintaining water levels in streams and wetlands, which supported fish populations and provided water for plants. When too many beavers were trapped, streams could change course or dry up, affecting the local environment. Some tribes saw their traditional food sources threatened. In addition, competition for furs sometimes led to conflicts between tribes, each wanting the best trapping grounds to trade with Europeans.

Disease continued to spread as well. Trappers and traders from Europe carried illnesses like smallpox, measles, or influenza, which Native Peoples had little resistance to. Trading posts, where many people gathered, could become hotspots for the spread of disease. This further weakened Native communities, who often had no access to effective treatments.

Trading Posts and Their Role

Trading posts were the heart of the fur trade. They were places where furs were collected, stored, and shipped out, and also where supplies were distributed. A typical post had a main storehouse, living quarters, and perhaps a blacksmith shop or small farm. Some, like Fort Vancouver, were quite large and became hubs for regional activity.

At a trading post, you might see people from many backgrounds—French-Canadian trappers, British clerks, Iroquois or Métis guides, Hawaiian laborers, and local tribal members. Many of these people married into local tribes, creating families of mixed heritage. Over time, a unique culture formed around these posts, blending Native traditions with European customs.

The Hudson's Bay Company, in particular, tried to manage relations with tribes in a way that kept the fur trade profitable. They did not want wars breaking out near their forts, because that would interrupt business. So they made treaties or agreements with tribal leaders. They also set rules about how many animals could be trapped in certain areas, hoping to prevent the extinction of the fur supply. However, enforcement was often weak, and local trappers sometimes ignored these rules if they believed they could make a bigger profit.

Competition and Conflict

Although the Hudson's Bay Company became the main power in the region after merging with the North West Company, other traders still tried to operate. American traders and smaller independent groups sometimes challenged the HBC's dominance. This led to tension on the rivers and in the backcountry. Some smaller companies tried to set up their own trading posts. Others sent out their own brigades of trappers. There were even episodes of sabotage, with rival trappers destroying each other's traps or trying to convince Native tribes not to trade with their competitors.

For the local tribes, these rivalries could be used to their advantage. By trading with different groups, they could sometimes negotiate better terms. For example, if one company offered more goods for fewer furs, the tribe might favor that company. This put pressure on the other company to offer equal or better deals. However, if a tribe sided too closely with one group, they risked angering another group or missing out on other opportunities.

Decline of the Sea Otter and Beaver Populations

After a few decades of intense hunting, sea otters along the Pacific Coast became scarce. Their numbers dropped sharply from Alaska to California. This meant the maritime fur trade that once thrived in coastal waters was no longer as profitable. Meanwhile, beaver populations in some river basins also faced heavy pressure. Trappers sometimes set hundreds of traps in a single valley, driving the beaver nearly to extinction in certain areas.

As these animals grew harder to find, the companies and independent trappers found it more expensive to operate. They had to travel farther into the wilderness to catch enough fur-bearing animals to make a profit. The cost of maintaining trading posts and supplying trappers rose. The fur trade was still strong, but the signs of decline were there.

Missionaries and Early Settlers Start Arriving

Around the same time, Christian missionaries from the United States and Europe began to arrive. They aimed to spread their faith among Native Peoples and also serve the spiritual needs of trappers and settlers. Though we will discuss missions and settlers more deeply in later chapters, their presence interacted with the fur trade in important ways. Mission stations sometimes offered rest or supplies to traveling trappers. Missions also introduced new ideas about agriculture and permanent settlement, which contrasted with the roving life of trappers.

A few settlers started to arrive, though very slowly at first. Some were retired trappers or company employees who decided to stay. They might set up small farms near trading posts to supply fresh produce to traders. These early settlers did not yet flood the region; that would come later. But their presence signaled that the Pacific Northwest was not only a place to collect furs but also a place to potentially live and farm.

The International Dispute Over Oregon Country

During the early 1800s, the Pacific Northwest was often called the "Oregon Country," a term that included present-day Washington, Oregon, Idaho, and parts of Montana and British Columbia. Both the United States and Great Britain claimed rights to it. After the War of 1812, the two nations agreed to a joint occupation, meaning citizens of both countries could settle and trade there. This arrangement worked for a while, largely because the region was remote and mostly filled with fur-trading activity.

The Hudson's Bay Company, which was British, had a strong presence through its network of posts. The United States, however, had fewer established posts after Fort Astoria was sold. Tensions remained low-key for a while. Yet, as American settlers grew in number, the question of who truly owned the land became more pressing. We will see in future chapters how this dispute eventually led to boundary agreements, but during the main fur trade era, business went on under this uneasy joint occupation.

Cultural Blending and Marriages

One unique aspect of the fur trade era was the blending of cultures. Fur traders came from many backgrounds: Scottish, English, French Canadian, Iroquois, and Hawaiian, among others. They worked alongside or married into local Native Tribes such as the Chinook, Yakama, or Spokane. Out of these unions came families who spoke multiple languages and practiced mixed traditions.

These families often lived at or near trading posts, forming small communities. Children grew up learning both their mother's Native language and their father's European language. They might adopt some European clothing styles but also learn traditional Native skills like basket weaving or canoe building. This cultural blending helped bridge gaps between European companies and Native tribes. However, as more settlers arrived later on, they sometimes looked down on these mixed-heritage families, leading to tension within the region.

Effects on the Land and People

By the mid-1800s, the fur trade was no longer as strong as it had been. Beaver populations were reduced in many areas, sea otters were rare, and new economic activities like farming and logging were beginning to gain importance. Native Peoples felt the impacts of ecological changes and ongoing disease outbreaks. Also, new laws and treaties would soon reshape their lives.

Still, the fur trade era left a lasting influence on Washington. It opened up travel routes, including river paths and mountain passes, that later settlers would use. Trading posts like Fort Vancouver became springboards for future towns. The knowledge of the land gained by trappers and Native guides helped shape future exploration and settlement. Despite the challenges and conflicts, this period marked a key step in Washington's shift from a land inhabited mainly by Native Tribes to a place where many different people would come and settle.

Looking Ahead

In this chapter, we saw how the fur trade dominated the Pacific Northwest for several decades. Companies like the Hudson's Bay Company built posts, hired trappers, and controlled much of the business. Native Tribes participated in the trade but also faced new diseases, disruptions to their environment, and changes to their economy. Rivalries between companies and nations simmered beneath the surface.

As we move forward, the fur trade will not vanish overnight, but its significance will begin to fade as missions and settlement increase. In the next chapters, we will explore how missionaries and early settlers shaped the land, bringing new religions, farming, and different perspectives on land ownership. We will also see how these changes stirred tensions between Native Peoples and newcomers, leading to conflicts and treaties that would define Washington's future.

CHAPTER 5

Missions and Early Settlers – Spreading Beliefs and Building Homes

---

In the early 1800s, the Pacific Northwest was still mostly home to Native Tribes and fur traders. However, word began to spread among church groups and families in the eastern United States about the opportunities out west. Some people wanted to travel there to teach religion to the Native Peoples. Others hoped to find good farmland and a fresh start. These travelers slowly made their way into the region we now call Washington, bringing new ideas, customs, and ways of life.

In this chapter, we will look at the arrival of missionaries, their interactions with Native Tribes, and how early settlers started building homes. Although their numbers were small at first, these newcomers helped shape the culture and landscape of Washington. We will also see how these changes affected the Native Peoples who had lived on this land for countless generations.

Religious Missions Come West

Protestant Missions

The first missionaries to arrive were often Protestant groups. They heard stories from explorers, trappers, and fur traders about the "unchurched" Native Peoples living near the Columbia River and other places in the Oregon Country (which included present-day Washington). Many of these missionaries felt a strong calling to bring Christianity to the Indigenous people. They also believed they could teach farming, reading, and writing, hoping to change Native lifestyles to match their own ideas.

Two well-known missionaries were Marcus and Narcissa Whitman. They traveled west in 1836 with another couple, Henry and Eliza Spalding. Their journey took them along what would later be known as the Oregon Trail. After a long and difficult trip, they arrived in the region near the Walla Walla River. The Whitmans set up their mission at Waiilatpu, close to the Cayuse Tribe's homeland. The Spaldings built their mission among the Nez Perce. These missions included a church, small homes, and farmland. The missionaries taught Native children in classrooms and held worship services.

Catholic Missions

Not long after Protestant missionaries arrived, Catholic priests also came to the Pacific Northwest. These Catholic missionaries often came from Canada or followed routes through the mountains used by the fur-trading companies. They, too, hoped to share their faith. Priests like Father Blanchet and Father Demers traveled widely, setting up chapels or small missions wherever they could. Later, other priests followed, sometimes staying at Hudson's Bay Company posts. Over time, Catholic missions appeared in many parts of the region, including near the Cowlitz River and in the Puget Sound area.

Catholic missionaries also offered religious services to French Canadian trappers who had settled in the area or married into local tribes. Because many of these trappers were already Catholic, the priests provided them with a familiar religious home. Native Peoples sometimes found the Catholic style of worship more in line with their own traditions of reverence, ritual, and community gatherings. This is not to say it was free from misunderstanding. Many cultural barriers still existed.

Daily Mission Life and Goals

Both Protestant and Catholic missionaries shared certain goals. They wanted to convert Native Peoples to Christianity, teach them how to read the Bible, and introduce new farming methods. Missions often had fenced gardens, orchards, or small fields where missionaries tried to grow crops like wheat, potatoes, and vegetables. They hoped that by showing Natives how to farm in the European style, they would encourage a more settled way of life. The missionaries believed this would bring what they saw as "improvement" and stability.

However, these efforts sometimes clashed with Native traditions. Many tribes had seasonal movements for hunting, fishing, or gathering. The idea of living in one place year-round and farming was foreign to them. Also, some missionaries insisted that Native converts abandon certain customs, spiritual beliefs, or ceremonies. This caused tension. While some individuals within the tribes were curious and willing to learn, others felt their traditions were under attack.

Early Settlers: Families Looking for Farmland

Missionaries were not the only newcomers. A growing number of families from the eastern United States began hearing about the fertile lands of the Pacific Northwest. The stories described a place with mild winters (compared to some parts of the Midwest), tall trees for building, and rivers full of fish. Some people thought they could create new communities, free from the crowded conditions or economic troubles back east.

Many of these families followed the Oregon Trail, which started around Missouri and stretched over 2,000 miles. The journey was harsh. People traveled in covered wagons pulled by oxen or mules. They faced storms, illness, accidents, and in some cases, conflicts with tribes along the way. Yet the promise of free or cheap land was enough to inspire these families to take the risk. By the 1840s and 1850s, more wagon trains were rolling west each year.

When these settlers arrived, they often passed through the missions, as missions were some of the few places offering shelter or information. Missionaries, in turn, saw them as an extension of the civilization they were trying to build. Some settlers decided to stay near mission sites, while others pressed on to the Willamette Valley (in present-day Oregon) or north into the Puget Sound region. Bit by bit, they formed the first farming communities.

Building Homes and Establishing Farms

Early settler homes were simple log cabins. Families cut down trees, shaped them into rough logs, and stacked them to form walls. They filled in the cracks with mud or moss. The roofs were often made of wooden shingles. Windows might be oiled paper rather than glass, at least at first. Over time, some settlers managed to buy or trade for glass windows. They also built small barns or shelters for animals. They grew gardens with corn, beans, peas, and whatever else they could manage in the local soil.

Settlers usually chose land near rivers or streams, so they would have water for crops, animals, and household use. They learned that coastal areas west of the Cascades were wetter, with heavy rain in winter. East of the mountains, the climate was drier, so irrigation became important. Each region posed its own challenges. In the forested west, settlers had to spend enormous effort clearing trees. In the eastern plains, they dealt with very cold winters and a shorter growing season. Yet farmland was cheap—or, in some cases, free if they stayed long enough on the land and improved it.

Neighbors often relied on each other. They would gather for barn raisings, where many people helped build a barn in a single day. Women might gather to sew or cook together, sharing knowledge of preserving food for winter. Children helped with chores from a young age. Life was tough, with few luxuries. Still, settlers found joy in family gatherings, music, or reading the Bible by candlelight.

Early Towns and Trading

As the number of settlers grew, small towns began to appear. A town usually started near a trading post or a mission. Perhaps a settler opened a store selling basic supplies: flour, sugar, tools, nails, and cloth. Then someone else might open a blacksmith shop to fix wagons or shoe horses. Over time, a schoolhouse might be built, then a church. Some of these towns remained tiny, while others grew quickly.

A few examples:

- **Olympia**: Located near the southern tip of Puget Sound, it became a stopping place for ships and travelers.
- **Vancouver**: This area near Fort Vancouver turned into a small settlement beyond just the Hudson's Bay Company post.

- **Steilacoom**: Known for being one of the earlier towns in the Puget Sound region, it had a fort, a store, and a few farms around it.

These small communities relied on boats or horseback for transportation. Roads were rough and not well-maintained. Rivers, sounds, and the ocean served as the primary highways, linking towns and missions together.

Relationship with Native Peoples

At first, many settlers tried to get along with local tribes. Some even learned a bit of the native languages, like Chinook Jargon, which was a trade language. They traded goods and sometimes hired Native labor for farming, fishing, or guiding. Likewise, some Native families found they could benefit from settler tools, metal pots, or wool blankets.

However, misunderstandings also arose. Settlers often assumed that if land looked unused or if it was outside a Native village, it could be claimed for farming. But Native concepts of land use did not match European-style ownership. Tribes might hunt or gather in areas seasonally and consider those places essential to their lives, even if no permanent village was there. As settlers fenced off fields, blocked traditional fishing spots, or cut down forests, Native communities felt displaced.

Missionaries sometimes tried to mediate. They taught about peaceful relations and fairness, at least in theory. But they also encouraged assimilation—urging Native Peoples to adopt European and Christian lifestyles. This push created further tensions, as it seemed to dismiss Native culture. Meanwhile, diseases like measles or smallpox continued to harm the tribes. As more settlers arrived, conflicts began to grow.

The Whitman Mission Incident

A turning point occurred at the Whitman Mission. Dr. Marcus Whitman was not just a preacher but also tried to provide medical care. In 1847, a severe measles outbreak struck both the settlers and the Cayuse Tribe near Waiilatpu. While many settlers recovered (since they often had some immunity), the Cayuse suffered heavy losses. They believed Dr. Whitman's medicine was not helping them; instead, they saw more of their people dying. Some members of the tribe suspected that Whitman was poisoning them, or at least failing them badly.

In their anger and fear, a group of Cayuse attacked the mission, killing Marcus and Narcissa Whitman along with several others. This tragedy became known as the Whitman Massacre. It shocked settlers throughout the region. The reaction among Americans was swift: more soldiers and settlers came, and many viewed the Cayuse and other tribes as dangerous. This event led to the Cayuse War, which we will discuss further in the next chapter. But it also marked a shift in how missionaries and settlers were seen by the tribes.

Effects on Future Missions

After the Whitman incident, missionaries realized that simply building missions and expecting Native Peoples to convert willingly could lead to deep misunderstandings. Some missions closed down. Others changed their approach, focusing more on basic education or humanitarian work and less on forced conversion. Tensions were high for many years. Missionaries from both Protestant and Catholic backgrounds remained, but they often found themselves caught in the middle of growing disputes between Native Tribes and the settlers who wanted more land.

Still, missions continued in some areas. Catholic priests founded a mission in the Yakima region. Others worked with the Spokane or the Coast Salish tribes around Puget Sound. They tried to learn local languages, create dictionaries, and even translate parts of the Bible. While their intentions might have been to help or "save" Native souls, they often disregarded the full value and richness of Native cultural beliefs.

Settlers Expand North and West

The Whitman incident did not stop the flow of settlers. In fact, the idea of the "Oregon Country" as a place of promise only grew. Newspapers back east printed stories—some true, some exaggerated—about tall fir trees, fish-filled rivers, and farmland ready to be claimed. People packed their wagons and headed west by the thousands, especially during the peak years of the Oregon Trail in the 1840s and early 1850s.

Some of these settlers were single men, but many were entire families. They established small towns around Puget Sound, where ships could dock, and in fertile river valleys in the interior. They introduced cattle, horses, sheep, and pigs, which sometimes roamed freely and grazed on land that tribes used for gathering roots or berries. Fences went up around homesteads, dividing the landscape in new ways. Logging camps appeared, cutting down ancient forests for lumber. Mills were built to saw the logs into boards.

For the settlers, these changes felt like progress—an example of making the land more "productive." But for the tribes, it could mean the loss of traditional food sources, spiritual places, and freedom to roam. Conflicts were brewing under the surface, and we will see in the next chapter how these tensions erupted into violence and forced treaties.

Early Territorial Government

As more Americans arrived, they pushed for organized government. At first, the entire Oregon Country was under a joint occupation agreement between the United States and Great Britain. But in 1846, the two nations settled the boundary issue by drawing the line at the 49th parallel. This gave the United States what is now Washington, Oregon, Idaho, and parts of Montana. The region that would become Washington was still part of the Oregon Territory at first.

In 1853, the United States Congress created the Washington Territory, separate from Oregon. It included the lands from the Pacific coast to the Rocky Mountains, though the boundaries changed later. Settlers in the newly formed Washington Territory elected officials and set up courts. Towns like Olympia and Steilacoom became territorial centers. This step marked the beginning of structured American governance in the region, further sidelining Native rights and claims to the land.

A Changing Culture

With missions, farms, and a growing territorial government, the culture of the region began to change rapidly. More schools opened, at least for settler children. Churches, both Protestant and Catholic, were established in young towns. Newspapers began to appear, spreading news and opinions. The sense of a "frontier society" took hold—a place where hard work and individual effort could shape one's destiny.

Despite this, not everyone found success. Some settlers discovered that clearing land was more difficult than expected, or that they were unprepared for the rainy Pacific winters. Illness, accidents, or conflicts with tribes could destroy a family's dream. Missionaries also struggled. They faced language barriers, health issues, and limited resources. Yet enough people persevered that the settler population steadily increased.

Lasting Effects of the Early Missions

These early missions did more than bring religion. They laid the groundwork for schools, agriculture, and future settlements. The missionary couples often started the first formal classes in the region, teaching both Native children and settler children how to read and write. They introduced new crops and fruit trees that eventually spread widely. Some missions became community centers, offering a place to gather, share news, or rest from traveling.

But the mission era also planted seeds of conflict. The push to change Native customs and the assumption that the land was open for settlement caused deep resentment among the tribes. Missionaries did not always understand Native traditions, nor did they appreciate how changes in land use might devastate older ways of life. As the number of settlers grew, the tribes felt a mounting pressure on their lands and resources.

CHAPTER 6

Conflict and Change – Tensions Between Native Tribes and Newcomers

By the mid-1800s, Washington's landscape was filled with a mix of Native communities, fur traders, missionaries, and a growing number of settlers. The peaceful exchanges that sometimes occurred gave way to rising tension. Different ideas about land use, broken promises, and outbreaks of violence all contributed to a climate of distrust. Eventually, open conflicts broke out between certain tribes and the newcomers.

In this chapter, we explore the causes and consequences of these tensions. We look at how treaties were formed, why they often failed, and how these events shaped the region's future. From the Cayuse War to later confrontations, the stage was set for dramatic changes in Native life and in the growth of American settlements across Washington Territory.

Early Signs of Trouble

Conflicts did not erupt overnight. There were warnings and signs along the way. As missions spread, some tribal leaders complained that their people were being pressured to adopt new religions and abandon traditional beliefs. Meanwhile, settlers claimed farmland in areas where tribes hunted, fished, or gathered. Over time, these disagreements intensified:

1. **Land Ownership Disputes**: Native Tribes did not typically mark land with fences or legal deeds. They understood boundaries based on natural features like rivers, mountains, or seasonal use areas. Settlers, on the other hand, believed in individual land ownership. They would often stake a claim, build a fence, and call the land their own, ignoring tribal use.

2. **Resource Competition**: Salmon, deer, and other wild foods had sustained tribes for centuries. Settlers brought livestock, changed rivers by building mills, and fenced off areas. This disrupted wildlife habitats. Some tribes found their usual food sources harder to get.
3. **Disease and Distrust**: Waves of smallpox, measles, and other diseases continued to harm Native communities. Many tribes saw newcomers as carriers of sickness, while settlers often blamed "unsanitary" Native living conditions for outbreaks. Misunderstandings added to the bitterness on both sides.

Against this backdrop, the Whitman Massacre in 1847 was a flashpoint. It led to the Cayuse War and set a pattern of violence, retribution, and fear that would mark the relationships between many tribes and settlers in the years to come.

The Cayuse War

Following the events at the Whitman Mission, American authorities demanded justice for the killings. They wanted the Cayuse to hand over those responsible. The Cayuse, in turn, felt that the settlers had brought disease that decimated their children and families. The conflict escalated into what is called the Cayuse War (1847–1855). Though not an all-out, continuous war, it involved a series of raids, skirmishes, and punitive expeditions.

U.S. militia forces and volunteers organized attacks on the Cayuse, destroying some of their villages and food supplies. The Cayuse tried to defend their lands, sometimes retreating into rugged areas to evade capture. Eventually, a small group of Cayuse leaders gave themselves up, hoping to save the rest of their people from constant warfare. Five men were executed by the territorial authorities for the Whitman killings. This did not truly resolve the deep issues at stake, but it ended the most active phase of the Cayuse War. Tensions, however, remained high.

Governor Isaac Stevens and the Treaty Process

As the Washington Territory began to organize its government, a key figure emerged: Isaac Stevens. Appointed as the first governor of the Washington Territory in 1853, he also served as the Superintendent of Indian Affairs for the region. This meant he was responsible for negotiating treaties with the tribes. Stevens believed in quickly settling the region with American families. He wanted to secure land for them and also prevent further violence by clarifying where tribes could live.

Between 1854 and 1855, Stevens met with various tribes to negotiate treaties. These gatherings, called treaty councils, were meant to define reservation boundaries and give the U.S. government the right to build roads, towns, and other infrastructure on former tribal lands. In return, tribes were promised certain payments, supplies, and guaranteed hunting and fishing rights.

Some tribes signed these treaties hoping it would protect at least a portion of their traditional lands and keep the peace. Others signed

54

because they felt they had no choice: the American settlers and soldiers were too numerous and powerful to resist. However, many of these treaties were poorly explained, rushed, or not fully understood by the Native leaders. Language barriers and cultural differences made it hard to grasp the full meaning of ceding land "forever" to another government.

The Walla Walla Council and Chief Kamiakin

One of the major treaty gatherings took place near Walla Walla in 1855. Representatives of several tribes attended, including the Yakama, Nez Perce, Cayuse, Umatilla, and Walla Walla. Governor Stevens led the American side. There, the Treaty of Walla Walla was negotiated, creating reservations for several tribes.

Chief Kamiakin of the Yakama was a key figure. He was wary of the newcomers and the treaty terms. Kamiakin spoke against ceding large portions of land. He wanted to keep sufficient territory for his people to hunt, fish, and live according to their traditions. Ultimately, however, the treaties were signed, partly due to pressures and assurances by Stevens. Not all tribal members agreed with the final decisions. This led to confusion and disagreement within the tribes themselves.

When the treaties were later broken or not fully honored—especially the promised boundaries and rights—anger boiled over. Many Native leaders felt betrayed. The stage was set for larger conflicts, including the Yakama War.

The Yakama War

Soon after the treaties were signed, settlers and miners began invading Yakama lands, ignoring the reservation boundaries. Gold had been discovered in the region, and a rush of prospectors poured in. They did not respect Yakama fishing sites or property. Some incidents of violence occurred between miners and Yakama members. In 1855, a Yakama chief was killed by miners, which led to retaliatory attacks by Yakama warriors. The U.S. Army then got involved.

The Yakama War (1855–1858) included multiple battles and raids. The Yakama, joined at times by other tribes, used their knowledge of the land to strike at military patrols and isolated settlements. The U.S. Army, for its part, organized campaigns to crush resistance and force the tribes onto reservations. Forts were built or reinforced around the region, and troops marched through tribal territories. Many Native families fled to safer areas, suffering from hunger and exposure.

In the end, the U.S. military's greater numbers and resources wore down the Yakama and their allies. Some tribal bands surrendered or were captured, and by 1858, the war largely ended. However, it did not bring lasting peace. The tribes were pushed onto reservations, losing control of millions of acres. Many Yakama people felt the treaties had been broken from the start, and their defeat only reinforced the view that the newcomers would keep taking land no matter what promises were made.

Other Regional Conflicts

The Yakama War was not the only conflict during this period. Other tribes also resisted or defended their lands when settlers moved in. In the Puget Sound area, tensions rose among the Nisqually, Puyallup, and other tribes. They, too, had signed treaties with Governor Stevens but soon found settlers occupying areas that had been promised for tribal use.

The Puget Sound War

Sparked by dissatisfaction with the Medicine Creek Treaty of 1854, the Puget Sound War (1855–1856) saw leaders like Chief Leschi of the Nisqually stand up against the United States. Leschi argued that the treaty had been unfairly negotiated, giving the tribes small reservations without good farmland. Fighting broke out, mostly in small skirmishes around the south Puget Sound region. Leschi was eventually captured and, after a controversial trial, executed. Many people later believed he had been unjustly convicted.

Conflicts with Coastal Tribes

Some coastal tribes, while not as directly affected by farmland seizure, still experienced clashes over fishing rights and resource control. As settlers established sawmills and ports, they restricted tribal access to shoreline areas, leading to arguments and sometimes violence. The U.S. government tried to move these tribes onto reservations as well, though the exact arrangements varied.

Broken Promises and Reservation Life

Even after treaties were signed, the promises within them were not always fulfilled. Payments to the tribes came late or not at all. The land set aside for reservations was sometimes smaller or poorer in quality than what was promised on the official treaty maps. Settlers continued to push into tribal territories to farm, mine, or log.

On the reservations, life was difficult. Tribes were expected to farm small plots of land, which many had never done before. They struggled with a lack of tools, seeds, and agricultural knowledge suited to the new environment. Disease remained a constant threat due to crowded conditions and limited medical help. Children were sometimes taken to mission schools where they were forbidden to speak their native languages or follow their cultural practices. This created deep wounds that would last for generations.

Resistance and Adaptation

Despite these challenges, many tribes found ways to resist or adapt. Some leaders traveled to Washington, D.C., to argue for their people's rights. Others used the American legal system, hiring lawyers to press land claims or protest treaty violations. Still, others kept their traditions alive in secret, passing songs, dances, and religious ceremonies from parents to children away from the eyes of the government.

A few tribal communities embraced certain new technologies or farming methods, hoping to create a better life under the tough circumstances. Some families started small businesses, selling crafts or services to settlers. Intermarriage with settlers or fur traders also created mixed-heritage families who navigated both worlds. Yet, the overall power balance favored the settlers, backed by the U.S. government and military forces.

The Military and the Growth of Forts

As conflicts grew, the U.S. Army built or expanded forts throughout Washington Territory. Examples include:

- **Fort Vancouver** (originally a Hudson's Bay Company post but later used by the U.S. Army)
- **Fort Steilacoom** near Puget Sound
- **Fort Walla Walla** in the southeastern region
- **Fort Colville** in the northeast

These forts served as bases for soldiers who patrolled the surrounding lands, responding to any sign of Native resistance. They also provided some settlers with a sense of security. However, they often represented a threat to the tribes. Some forts became centers for negotiations or distribution of government rations. Others were simply strongholds that enforced the new order.

Changing Landscape of Power

By the late 1850s and early 1860s, most tribes in Washington had been forced onto reservations or had signed treaties limiting their movements. The U.S. government shifted its focus to other matters, including the Civil War (1861–1865). During the Civil War, troop levels in Washington Territory were sometimes reduced, but the overall pattern of settling the land and confining tribes continued. New settlers kept coming, establishing more farms, mills, and towns.

This shift meant that the tribes were no longer seen as major threats. Indeed, the American view was that they were now mostly under control. Some tribal members continued to fight in small-scale actions, but large organized resistance was hard to sustain. With farmland and new industries growing, the territory was moving toward eventual statehood.

Long-Term Impacts of Conflict and Treaties

For Native Peoples, the treaties and wars of the mid-1800s had long-lasting effects. Much of their ancestral land was lost, and many cultural traditions were restricted or suppressed. The reservation system isolated tribes, and government agents often tried to force assimilation. Children were sent to boarding schools where they had to speak English and follow Christian practices. Many families suffered from poverty, loss of identity, and discrimination.

For settlers and the U.S. government, these conflicts opened more land for development. The farmland, forests, and waterways of Washington became sites for agriculture, logging, fishing, and eventually mining and industry. The territory could expand without the same fear of organized Native resistance. Towns grew into cities, and railroads would soon connect distant points. While this was celebrated as progress by many newcomers, it came at a huge cost to the original inhabitants.

Reflection on Choices and Consequences

Looking back, historians often note that there were missed opportunities for peaceful coexistence. If the government and settlers had recognized Native land rights and worked out fair agreements, much bloodshed might have been avoided. If treaties had been honored in good faith, tribes might have retained larger portions of their homeland, preserving more of their traditions. But the desire for land, resources, and expansion overshadowed these possibilities.

At the same time, it is important to acknowledge that some tribal leaders tried to negotiate, compromise, or adopt certain new ways. They saw that change was inevitable and hoped to guide that change to benefit their people. Others chose resistance, believing that giving up their land was too great a sacrifice. Both paths were filled with hardships and uncertain outcomes.

A Foundation for Future Relations

These mid-1800s conflicts set the stage for how Washington would develop socially, politically, and economically. The reservation system and the ongoing push for statehood were direct outcomes of this period. The treaties signed then still have legal implications today, especially regarding fishing, hunting, and land rights. Many tribal lawsuits in the modern era trace their legal rights back to language in those 19th-century treaties.

Despite the violence and broken promises, tribes found ways to keep their cultures alive. They preserved stories, songs, and ceremonies. They remembered their connection to the land and passed on their heritage to future generations. Meanwhile, American settlers built the infrastructure and communities that would eventually transform the territory into a state.

Looking Ahead

In this chapter, we have seen how tensions between Native Tribes and newcomers grew into conflicts and wars. We learned about the role of treaties, leaders like Isaac Stevens and Chief Kamiakin, and the struggle for land and resources. We also looked at how forts and the U.S. Army shaped the balance of power. While the immediate outcome favored the settlers, it left a profound mark on the tribes.

In the next chapters, we will examine more aspects of early Washington life, including how the Oregon Trail and westward movement brought even more settlers, how Washington became a formal U.S. Territory, and how industries such as logging, fishing, and farming started to take root. These topics will show how the conflicts and treaties of this period paved the way for dramatic changes in the land, the people, and the economy of Washington in the years that followed.

CHAPTER 7

The Oregon Trail and Westward Movement – Settlers Flood Into the Region

By the 1840s, many people in the eastern United States were hearing stories about the abundant farmland of the Oregon Country—an area that included modern-day Washington, Oregon, Idaho, and parts of Montana and Wyoming. Tales spread of wide prairies, tall forests, and mild weather, creating a strong desire for land and a new life. Families began packing their belongings into covered wagons and setting out on what came to be called the Oregon Trail. Although much of this migration initially targeted the Willamette Valley in present-day Oregon, a sizeable number of these settlers turned north into the lands that became Washington. The Oregon Trail became a key factor in the surge of newcomers who would forever change the region's character.

In this chapter, we explore the Oregon Trail's origins, the journey itself, and how it shaped Washington's early growth. We look at the motivations behind the movement, the daily life of travelers, and the impact this wave of settlers had on local Native Tribes, missions, and trading posts.

The Call of the West

Economic Hardship in the East

During the 1830s and 1840s, parts of the United States were hit by economic depressions. Farms in places like Ohio or Missouri could suffer from overused soil or competition from larger plantations.

Factories in eastern cities laid off workers, and many families found it hard to get by. Meanwhile, newspapers and land agents promised nearly free farmland out west, where crops supposedly grew easily, and wide rivers teemed with fish. This dream of prosperity was called "Oregon Fever."

Manifest Destiny

Another idea fueling westward movement was "Manifest Destiny." This was the belief that the United States had a God-given right—some even said a duty—to expand its territory all the way to the Pacific Ocean. Though this notion often ignored or dismissed the rights of Native Peoples and existing Spanish or British claims, it inspired thousands of Americans to set their sights on Oregon Country. They hoped not only to improve their own lives but also to spread American values and culture across the continent.

The Route of the Oregon Trail

The Oregon Trail was not a single, fixed path at first. It was a network of trails starting from towns along the Missouri River—places like Independence or St. Joseph in Missouri. From there, wagon trains headed west across the Great Plains, passing forts like Fort Kearny in Nebraska and Fort Laramie in Wyoming. They crossed the Rocky Mountains through the South Pass in present-day Wyoming, then moved on through rough landscapes and river valleys, including portions of Idaho, before reaching the Columbia River region. Some travelers turned northwest into what would become Washington. Others continued southwest toward the Willamette Valley.

This journey spanned roughly 2,000 miles and could take four to six months, depending on weather, river conditions, and the health of people and animals. Timing was crucial. Most wagon trains aimed to leave in late April or May to avoid muddy spring roads and arrive before winter snows blocked mountain passes.

Preparing for the Journey

Families saved money for months or even years to buy wagons, animals, food, and supplies. Oxen were the most common draft animals, as they were strong and relatively cheap. Some used mules, which were faster but more expensive. Horses were less common because they required more care and were easily stolen or lost. Travelers packed flour, bacon, beans, coffee, dried fruit, salt, and other staples to feed themselves during the journey. Women often brought seeds or cuttings of plants, hoping to grow them in their new homes.

People also brought tools like axes, shovels, and spare wagon parts. Clothes were important, but most travelers had only a few changes of clothing. A typical wagon might also hold bedding, cooking gear, and personal items such as Bibles, diaries, or small family keepsakes. If it was too heavy, travelers had to lighten the load along the trail, leaving precious possessions by the roadside.

Life on the Trail

Daily Routine

Travelers usually woke before sunrise to gather the oxen or mules, eat a quick breakfast, and hitch up the wagons. They aimed to travel about 15 miles a day if the terrain was good and no problems arose. At noon, they might stop briefly to rest the animals and have a cold meal. By late afternoon or early evening, they set up camp near a water source, if possible. Women prepared supper, while men tended to the animals or scouted for any signs of trouble. Children helped collect firewood or played around the wagons.

The wagon train often formed a circle at night, which provided some protection against theft, wandering animals, or potential attacks. People slept in tents, under the wagons, or inside them if there was room. Once or twice a week, if conditions allowed, they rested for an entire day. They used that time to wash clothes, make repairs, or simply recover from the constant strain of travel.

Hardships and Dangers

Travel on the Oregon Trail was fraught with dangers:

1. **Disease**: Cholera was especially feared. It could spread quickly through a wagon train, causing severe dehydration and death. Other illnesses such as dysentery, measles, or smallpox also took a toll.
2. **Accidents**: Wagon wheels could break, animals could stampede, or travelers might drown while crossing rivers. People occasionally fell under wagon wheels or were injured by firearms.
3. **Weather**: Heat and dust in the plains, fierce storms, and early snows in the mountains posed serious risks. Flooded rivers could halt progress for days.

4. **Scarce Food and Water**: The trail crossed deserts and other arid regions where grass for the animals was sparse. Families rationed their supplies carefully, but hunger was not uncommon.

Many travelers arrived at their destination weakened, with broken wagons, dead animals, and smaller families than when they set out. Yet the promise of good land drove them onward.

Meeting Native Peoples Along the Trail

Contrary to what some accounts at the time suggested, most encounters between wagon trains and Native Peoples along the Oregon Trail were peaceful. Tribes like the Pawnee, Shoshone, and others often served as guides or traded food for useful items. However, misunderstandings or hostility did happen. Some tribes, upset about wagon trains scaring away game or using up resources, charged tolls or demanded payment for crossing their lands.

As travelers approached the Columbia Plateau, they might pass near the lands of the Cayuse, Umatilla, and other tribes who had already faced disruptions from fur traders, missionaries, and previous waves of settlers. By the 1850s, tension between settlers and some tribes was growing. The arrival of more and more wagon trains only added stress to these relations, sometimes leading to conflict. Yet, in most cases, trade and cautious cooperation kept violence at bay, at least until the numbers of settlers became overwhelming.

Reaching Oregon Country and Spreading into Washington

When settlers finally reached the western end of the trail, many settled in the Willamette Valley of present-day Oregon. Others, hearing of good land in the Puget Sound region or along the Columbia River in what is now Washington, decided to keep traveling north.

- **Puget Sound**: Those who ventured toward Puget Sound found dense forests, plenty of rain, and a moderate climate. They set up homesteads near waterways for easier travel and trade.
- **Columbia Basin**: Farther east, on the plateau, the land was drier. Settlers there discovered they had to irrigate their fields, especially if they wanted to grow large crops. Still, they found the open space appealing.

In either case, new arrivals built cabins, cleared land, and planted crops. Some found already-established missions or trading posts where they could get supplies. Others had to rely on their own skills until a store or neighbor appeared closer by.

Effect on Missions and Trading Posts

The steady stream of settlers transformed existing missions and trading posts. Missions that once focused mainly on converting Native Peoples found themselves offering shelter and guidance to weary wagon trains. Some missionaries saw it as part of their duty to welcome Christian families, while others worried that the influx of newcomers would cause additional stress and conflicts with the tribes.

Trading posts, originally set up for the fur trade, saw a new market in the settlers. Owners began stocking more goods suited to farmers: plows, seeds, cooking pots, cloth for making clothes, and so on. Sawmills sprang up to supply lumber for building homes and barns. Local tribes were sometimes left on the margins of this new economy, unless they adapted by providing labor, selling fish or game, or working as guides.

In some cases, the arrival of large groups of settlers caused friction with the missionaries. The mission lands might be overrun with wagons, animals, and unplanned settlements. The missionaries, who had tried to maintain careful relations with tribes, now found that events were out of their control. The Oregon Trail had essentially burst open the door to massive change.

Tensions with Native Tribes

By the time the Oregon Trail migration was in full swing, many tribes in Washington had already experienced broken treaties or were suffering from disease outbreaks. The sheer number of settlers traveling through or moving in made it almost impossible for Native leaders to maintain control over their lands. Rivers once used by tribes for fishing became clogged with newly built mills or dams. Traditional hunting grounds were fenced or claimed by homesteaders.

The U.S. government tried to manage this by drafting treaties and creating reservations, but we have already seen in earlier chapters that these treaties were often rushed, misunderstood, or ignored by settlers. Some tribes fought to resist further incursions, leading to conflicts that shaped Washington's early development. The Oregon Trail migration played a direct role in these clashes, as it was one of the main channels bringing settlers into contact with Native communities.

Growth of Settlements and Infrastructure

New Towns and Roads

Wherever settlers gathered, small towns often sprouted. Entrepreneurs opened shops to sell supplies to incoming wagon trains or to local farmers. Blacksmiths offered repair services for broken wagons. Sawmills provided lumber for cabins, barns, and eventually more permanent structures. As communities expanded, rough roads were built or improved, making it easier for more wagons to come. Ferries or bridges appeared over rivers, reducing the dangers of crossing.

The desire for better transport led to calls for official territorial governments to support road-building and other public works. This, in turn, set the stage for Washington to separate from Oregon Territory and become a territory of its own. By this time, the population had grown enough to demand greater representation in government.

Communication and Mail

The influx of settlers also fueled the need for mail routes, telegraph lines (once that technology arrived in the region), and stagecoach services. People wanted to stay in touch with relatives and friends back east, telling them about the journey, the new land, and any opportunities. These letters often encouraged even more migration. Over the years, what began as a trickle of wagons turned into a major wave, with thousands of new arrivals each season.

End of the Oregon Trail Era

By the late 1860s, railroads began to expand across the country. Though they would not reach Washington in a major way for some time, the idea of traveling by train made the wagon trek less appealing. Also, the best farm lands in some areas had already been claimed, forcing newcomers to look further away from established routes. Over time, the Oregon Trail lost its importance as the primary path west. Instead, new roads and eventually railway lines guided settlers to Washington and other western states.

Still, the memory of the Oregon Trail lived on. It became part of the region's story: brave pioneers crossing a continent in search of a better life. Their struggles and hopes shaped much of the cultural identity of the Pacific Northwest, including Washington.

Lasting Impact on Washington

The Oregon Trail was instrumental in turning Washington from a sparsely settled territory of fur traders, missionaries, and scattered Native communities into a region steadily filling with American settlers. These pioneers established farms, towns, and local governments. Their presence forced significant changes in the lives of Native Peoples, disrupted ecosystems, and opened the door to more commerce and eventual statehood.

Families who took the trail often sent word back home, praising the mild climate of Puget Sound or the rich soil of the Columbia River valleys. This publicity spurred even more migration, creating a cycle of growth that would continue well into the late 1800s. The path may not have been easy—thousands lost their lives on the route—but for those who survived, the reward was a chance to claim land and build a new future in a place they believed to be full of promise.

Looking Ahead

With the rise in settlers brought by the Oregon Trail and other migration routes, Washington's population increased steadily. People began setting up local governments and organizing towns more formally. Conflicts with Native Tribes continued, but the governmental framework to manage disputes and distribute land was growing more complex.

In the next chapter, we will explore how Washington officially became a separate U.S. Territory, carving out its own identity and legal structures. The establishment of territorial government laid the groundwork for law and order on a frontier that had known mostly informal arrangements up to that point. As we will see, creating a territory brought new officials, a legislature, and more direct involvement from the federal government—all of which would shape Washington's path to statehood years later.

CHAPTER 8

Washington Becomes a Territory – Law and Order on the Frontier

By the early 1850s, the region that would become Washington was changing rapidly. Missions had been established, fur trading posts dotted the land, and more settlers were arriving each year—especially due to the Oregon Trail migration. At first, these new arrivals fell under the jurisdiction of the Oregon Territory, created in 1848. But the area north of the Columbia River felt distant from the territorial capital in the Willamette Valley. Settlers in present-day Washington wanted a government of their own to address local concerns.

This chapter examines the process by which Washington split from Oregon to become its own territory in 1853. We look at the main players involved, the challenges of organizing a frontier government, and the impact this change had on the region's development. We also delve into how the establishment of law and order shaped daily life for both settlers and Native Peoples, setting the stage for future conflicts and agreements.

The Push for Separation

Geographic and Cultural Differences

In the early 1850s, settlers north of the Columbia River realized their needs were not always met by the Oregon Territorial government centered near Salem. Travel to the territorial capital was long and difficult, requiring either a journey by boat on the Columbia and Willamette Rivers or a trip over rough wagon roads. Moreover, the climate and geography of the Puget Sound region differed from the Willamette Valley. Settlers in Washington needed roads, schools, and laws tailored to their unique environment.

As the population grew around Puget Sound, in areas like Olympia, Steilacoom, and Vancouver (near the old Hudson's Bay post), community leaders began lobbying in favor of forming a new territory. They sent petitions to the U.S. Congress, pointing out that the region had enough settlers to justify a separate government. Some also argued that this would make administration of Native affairs simpler, as negotiations with tribes like the Yakama, Nisqually, and others would be handled by officials closer to the affected areas.

Political Maneuvering

Leaders such as Michael T. Simmons, who founded settlements near Olympia, and other local pioneers joined forces to push for separation. They wrote letters, gathered signatures, and enlisted the support of influential figures in Oregon Territory. Eventually, Oregon's territorial representatives also backed the idea, recognizing that dividing the large territory might help them govern more effectively.

In 1853, Congress agreed to create the Washington Territory. The name honored George Washington, the first President of the United States. The new territory included all land west of the Rocky Mountains and north of the Columbia River (plus an area that is now part of northern Idaho and western Montana). The remaining portion to the south stayed as Oregon Territory, which was on its own path toward statehood (achieved in 1859).

Isaac Stevens: The First Territorial Governor

When Washington Territory was formed, President Franklin Pierce appointed Isaac I. Stevens as the first governor. Stevens was a controversial figure. Not only was he governor, but he also served as Superintendent of Indian Affairs. This dual role gave him tremendous authority over both the settler population and Native Tribes. Stevens arrived in Olympia in late 1853, eager to organize the territory and fulfill his mandates.

Stevens also had another task: surveying possible railroad routes across the northern part of the United States. He believed a transcontinental railroad passing through Washington would spur growth and strengthen American claims against British interests to the north. Balancing these duties was challenging, but Stevens worked tirelessly, often traveling to hold treaty negotiations or to explore passable routes through the mountains.

Setting Up a Territorial Government

Territorial Capital in Olympia

One of the first decisions was selecting a territorial capital. Olympia, a small community at the southern tip of Puget Sound, was chosen. The town had a strategic location near waterways and was already a gathering place for new settlers. Though modest in size, Olympia now became the center of political life in Washington Territory. A simple wooden structure served as the first Capitol building, hosting legislative meetings.

Settlers from across the territory flocked to Olympia when the legislature was in session to discuss matters like road building, property laws, and education. Newspapers began publishing regular updates on legislative decisions, helping unify far-flung communities that had felt isolated. Despite rough travel conditions, the territorial government slowly took shape.

Establishing Laws and Courts

The new territorial legislature was responsible for writing basic laws—covering everything from property rights to crimes like theft or assault. They formed judicial districts, allowing traveling judges (circuit judges) to hold court sessions in different parts of the territory. This was essential on a frontier where disputes over land boundaries, unpaid debts, or personal conflicts could quickly escalate.

Sheriffs and constables were appointed to enforce the law. Jails were built in some towns, though they were often small and not very secure. Overall, the territory struggled with a shortage of trained lawyers, judges, and law enforcement officers. Still, the people were happy to have a system in place, compared to the more informal arrangements before territorial status.

Interactions with Native Tribes

Treaty Negotiations

As mentioned in earlier chapters, Isaac Stevens played a major role in negotiating treaties with Native Tribes. He aimed to quickly secure land for settlers and define reservation boundaries so that conflicts would be reduced. From 1854 to 1855, Stevens held several treaty councils, including the Medicine Creek Treaty (near Puget Sound) and the Walla Walla Council (which led to multiple treaties affecting tribes like the Yakama, Walla Walla, and Umatilla).

These treaties promised tribes specific reservations and guaranteed fishing and hunting rights. In return, tribes ceded vast amounts of their traditional lands to the United States. Settlers were then free to homestead these newly "opened" lands, and the territorial government could plan roads, towns, and rail lines with fewer legal obstacles. Many tribal leaders signed under pressure, not fully aware of the long-term effects.

Growing Conflicts

The signing of treaties did not end disagreements. Many tribes realized that settlers were moving onto lands more quickly than anticipated. Government annuities (payments in goods or money) were often late or insufficient. In some cases, the promised reservation boundaries were not respected by local officials or settlers eager for prime farmland.

These problems led to further conflicts, such as the Yakama War, the Puget Sound War, and smaller skirmishes around the territory. The territorial government had to call on volunteer militias or request federal troops to handle crises. This fueled resentment on both sides: settlers saw tribes as obstacles to progress, while tribes felt cheated and displaced. The new government structures faced a massive challenge keeping peace amid rapid changes.

Expanding the Economy

Agriculture and Logging

With more formal government in place, settlers felt more confident about investing in farms and businesses. Agriculture began to boom, especially in the fertile valleys along rivers and around the Puget Sound lowlands. Wheat, oats, and other grains were planted. Cattle ranching also took off, providing meat and dairy for local consumption. Some areas experimented with fruit orchards, trying apples, pears, and plums.

Logging quickly became a major industry. The towering Douglas firs and cedars of Western Washington were in high demand for building ships, homes, and even entire cities. Sawmills popped up near ports, turning raw logs into boards and shingles. This lumber was shipped to San Francisco and other growing towns on the West Coast. Although the fur trade continued in a smaller capacity, it was now overshadowed by these new economic pursuits.

Fishing and Canning

Salmon runs in the rivers of Washington were legendary. Native Tribes had relied on salmon for generations, but now settlers and businesses also saw an opportunity. They built fish traps, nets, and eventually canneries to preserve salmon for shipment. This industry employed many workers, including Native peoples at certain sites, though it drastically impacted the fish populations over time. Early canneries laid the foundation for the large commercial fishing operations that would come later.

Towns and Roads

Infrastructure Development

The territorial government recognized that poor transportation limited economic growth. Thus, it funded the improvement of wagon roads connecting towns like Olympia, Steilacoom, and Vancouver. In Eastern Washington, settlers clamored for better roads to ferry their wheat and other produce. Private investors sometimes built toll roads or ferries, charging fees to travelers.

Harbor improvements were also made. Docks and piers in Puget Sound towns allowed for the loading of lumber, fish, and farm products onto ships bound for California or even Hawaii. Small steamships began operating in the 1850s and 1860s, making travel by water faster and more reliable than before.

Growth of Settlements

As roads and docks improved, more settlers arrived. Some towns like Olympia, Steilacoom, and Port Townsend grew steadily, becoming hubs of local trade. In Eastern Washington, Walla Walla developed as an agricultural center. Gold discoveries in nearby Idaho brought prospectors through Washington, increasing business for local merchants.

Hotels, general stores, and blacksmith shops sprang up to cater to travelers. Churches and schools followed, often supported by missionary organizations or local community funds. The population remained scattered, but each decade saw more families claiming land, planting crops, and establishing permanent roots. The shape of Washington's future was taking form as a place not just of trade and missions, but of organized farms, towns, and industries.

Challenges in Law Enforcement and Justice

Frontier Realities

Despite the formal government, the Washington Territory still had a frontier character. Law enforcement was thin. Sheriffs and deputies covered huge areas, sometimes taking days to respond to a crime. When arrests were made, jails were not always secure. This led to instances of vigilante justice, where settlers took the law into their own hands—sometimes lynching suspects without a fair trial.

For Native peoples accused of crimes (or who accused settlers), the situation was especially unclear. Tribal leaders had their own justice systems, but those held no authority over American settlers. Territorial courts frequently failed to understand or honor tribal legal traditions. This created an uneven system, often favoring settlers and punishing tribal members harshly.

Territorial vs. Federal Power

The Washington Territory had a governor, a legislature, and courts, but it also remained under the oversight of the federal government. Congress could overturn certain territorial laws or dismiss governors. The federal army could be brought in if territorial militias seemed too weak. This mixed authority sometimes led to confusion or power struggles. Governors came and went relatively quickly, each bringing new ideas. Meanwhile, local leaders tried to assert control where they could.

The San Juan Islands Dispute

An interesting episode of early Washington Territory history was the boundary dispute over the San Juan Islands, located between Vancouver Island (British territory) and the mainland of Washington. Both the United States and Britain claimed these islands after the 1846 treaty that set the 49th parallel as the border. The language of the treaty was unclear about which channel separated the islands from the mainland, leading to a standoff known as the "Pig War" in 1859.

When an American settler shot a British-owned pig on San Juan Island, tensions flared. Both sides sent troops to the island. Governor Stevens and territorial officials insisted the islands belonged to Washington Territory. Britain argued they were part of its colony. Fortunately, actual fighting never happened, and a peaceful joint occupation lasted until the dispute was settled by arbitration in 1872 in favor of the United States. The so-called "Pig War" showed how uncertain the borders could be and how fragile peace remained during this period.

Education and Cultural Life

Early Schools

As the territory formed, settlers pressed for schools. Families wanted their children to learn reading, writing, arithmetic, and basic American values. Some communities organized small one-room schoolhouses, hiring a teacher for a few months of the year. Textbooks were scarce and often second-hand, but the children learned from whatever was available. Missionary schools still operated in certain areas, especially on or near reservations, though Native children were often pressured to give up their language and customs there.

Newspapers and Churches

Printing presses arrived in the territory, allowing for the creation of local newspapers. These papers, such as The Columbian in Olympia, spread news about legislative sessions, new road openings, arrivals of ships, and local events. They played a key role in keeping the scattered population informed. Churches grew in number, with Protestant and Catholic congregations establishing permanent buildings and offering Sunday services. Some churches doubled as community centers for social gatherings.

A Path Toward Statehood

During the 1850s and 1860s, Washington Territory slowly built the institutions it needed to function independently: a legislature, courts, schools, and more. However, full statehood would not come until 1889. Several factors delayed that process, including the relatively small population in some parts of the territory and the turmoil of the American Civil War (1861–1865). Also, the federal government had to balance admitting new states that could shift the balance of power in Congress, especially concerning issues like slavery prior to the Civil War.

Nevertheless, the foundation was set. Each decade brought more settlers, more industries, and more infrastructure. Towns expanded, farmland increased, and the region's ties to the rest of the country grew stronger. The frontier was still rough and unpredictable, but law and order had taken root through territorial governance. By the end of the 1860s, Washington was well on its way to becoming a fully integrated part of the United States.

Native Tribes Under Territorial Rule

For Native Tribes, the creation of the Washington Territory was a mixed event. While some leaders hoped a closer, local government might address their concerns more fairly, the speed of settler expansion only increased. Treaties led to reservations, and reservations often meant restricted movement and limited resources. The territorial government generally prioritized the interests of settlers and businesses, leaving tribes to appeal to federal agents or courts far away if they felt cheated.

Conflicts continued in various forms, from violent flare-ups to legal battles. The U.S. Army enforced the new laws and boundaries, placing more pressure on tribal communities. Disease, displacement, and the loss of traditional lands took a heavy toll. By the 1860s, many tribes were struggling to survive under conditions that were very different from the life their ancestors had known.

Legacy of the Territorial Era

The territorial period left a deep imprint on Washington. It was a time of rapid change, setting the stage for the eventual push for statehood. Roads, schools, and government institutions provided a framework for future growth. The logging and farming industries that began in this era would remain central to Washington's economy for decades. Cities like Olympia, Seattle, Tacoma, and Spokane would emerge from these small pioneer communities, aided by transportation routes first planned in territorial days.

On the other hand, this era also established patterns of imbalance and conflict. Tribes were confined to reservations and often denied their full treaty rights. The environment began to suffer from unchecked resource extraction, from overfishing to clear-cut logging. While these issues would carry on into modern times, their roots can be found in the decisions and policies of the territorial government.

CHAPTER 9

Growing Towns and New Industries – Logging, Fishing, and Farming

---

In the years following the establishment of Washington Territory in 1853, many changes swept across the region. Towns began to grow into more organized communities, and new industries took root. Logging, fishing, and farming emerged as the cornerstone activities that helped early settlers earn a living. As the population increased, local businesses opened, shipping routes expanded, and more people found their way to the forests, rivers, and coasts of Washington.

In this chapter, we will explore how logging became a powerhouse industry, how fishing supported both local needs and far-away markets, and how farming spread across different parts of the territory. We will also look at how these industries shaped the character of the growing towns, as well as the challenges faced by workers, families, and the land itself.

A Time of Rapid Growth

Settlers and Town Formation

By the late 1850s and early 1860s, settlers arrived in larger numbers, seeking opportunities in Washington. Some were families moving from the eastern states, while others were single men looking for work in logging camps or at sawmills. In towns such as Olympia, Steilacoom, and Vancouver, businesses sprang up to serve these newcomers. General stores sold tools, clothing, and household goods. Blacksmith shops fixed wagons and shoed horses. Boarding houses offered simple meals and sleeping areas to workers passing through.

Because the territory was still young, most of these towns were small. Dirt roads and wooden sidewalks (if any) lined the streets. Houses were often made of rough-hewn lumber or logs. A handful of churches appeared, representing different Christian denominations. Schools were usually one-room buildings where a single teacher handled all ages and subjects. Newspapers spread the latest happenings, from political news to stories of local heroes who had wrestled bears or survived river crossings.

Some individuals amassed enough wealth to build bigger homes or open larger stores. Others lived day to day, hoping to earn a decent wage in logging camps or fishing canneries. Tensions over land ownership with local Native Tribes remained, but the fast pace of settlement continued. Each new farm, mill, or store added to the sense that Washington was on the verge of even bigger things.

The Rise of Logging

Vast Forests and Timber Demand

One of Washington's greatest natural treasures was its enormous forests. Towering Douglas fir, western red cedar, and hemlock covered much of the western part of the territory. These trees often grew to incredible heights and widths. Early explorers and settlers marveled at them, realizing that they could be turned into valuable lumber for construction. Demand for timber was high, especially in fast-growing cities like San Francisco, where fires and constant building projects created a need for quality wood.

Logging Camps and Techniques

Logging in these early years was grueling, dangerous work. Men used axes, crosscut saws, and wedges to fell massive trees. It could take several men many hours to cut through a single trunk, which might measure several feet in diameter. Workers had to be mindful of "widow-makers"—branches that could snap and fall from great heights without warning.

Once a tree was down, loggers trimmed the branches, cut the trunk into manageable sections, and hauled the logs to nearby rivers or rails (where they existed) to move them. In the earliest days, oxen pulled the logs along rough "skid roads," which were tracks greased with animal fat to help the logs slide more easily. Later, teams of horses and mules were also used. The logs were often floated downriver to sawmills, which turned them into boards, shingles, and timbers.

Logging camps were basic. Men slept in bunkhouses, sometimes made of logs themselves. Food was simple—beans, salted pork, biscuits, and coffee. Injuries were common: saw cuts, falling trees, or smashed limbs. In the rainy season, camps became muddy and cold. Still, for many workers, the wages were higher than they might find elsewhere, and the adventure of frontier life held a strong appeal.

Sawmills and Export

Sawmills popped up along waterways, especially near Puget Sound. The location was crucial: mills needed a steady supply of logs, which came in by river or floated across the Sound, and easy shipping routes to transport the finished lumber. Steam-powered saws became more common in the late 1850s and early 1860s, increasing production. Mill owners cut boards and beams for local building needs, but they also shipped large amounts to California, Oregon, and even Hawaii.

Ship captains loaded lumber onto schooners and steamers, bringing money and more settlers back to Washington on return trips. Towns with busy mills could grow quickly, as workers spent wages at local shops and families settled nearby. This cycle helped transform sleepy coastal areas into thriving communities.

Fishing: From Traditional Harvest to Commercial Enterprise

Salmon as a Staple

Long before settlers arrived, salmon was a staple food for many Native Tribes in Washington. Rivers like the Columbia, the Snake, and countless smaller streams teemed with salmon during their spawning runs. Tribes had built sophisticated fish traps, weirs, and nets to catch enough salmon for their families and for trade. When settlers came, they were amazed at the abundance of fish and saw an opportunity for profit.

The Growth of Canneries

By the 1860s and 1870s, enterprising individuals set up small canneries along major rivers and coastal areas. These canneries processed salmon, packing the meat in tins to ship it long distances. At first, the canning process was done by hand: workers cleaned and cut the fish, filled the cans, and heated them over large boiling vats to seal them. Eventually, some mechanical aids were introduced, but it remained labor-intensive work.

Many cannery workers were Native people who knew the best ways to handle salmon. Some were Chinese immigrants hired to clean and pack fish, while others were settlers' families looking for seasonal work. Pay was usually low, and conditions were harsh—strong smells, slippery floors, and high heat in the boiling rooms. Yet, canned salmon found a solid market both locally and in distant cities, so the industry grew.

Fishing Methods and Challenges

While tribes continued traditional fishing methods, commercial operations relied on large nets, fish wheels, or traps placed near riverbanks. Fish wheels were rotating devices powered by the flow of the river, scooping up salmon as they passed by. Traps, anchored to pilings in shallow waters, funneled fish into enclosed areas for easy harvest. These methods allowed canneries to catch vast numbers of salmon.

Over time, settlers noticed the salmon runs became smaller in certain rivers, likely due to overfishing and the destruction of spawning grounds. Logging also contributed by causing erosion and sediment that choked streambeds. Environmental awareness was limited, so few regulations existed to protect salmon habitats. Still, the fishing industry thrived, fueling local economies and attracting more workers to Washington's rivers and coasts.

Farming in Varied Climates

Western Washington: Rain and Forest Clearing

For many settlers, farming was the ultimate goal. They wanted to own land, raise crops, and build a stable life for their families.

Western Washington had plenty of rainfall, which was good for certain crops but also meant thick forests that had to be cleared before fields could be planted. Cutting and burning stumps was backbreaking labor, and it could take years to clear enough land for a decent-sized farm.

Still, once the land was cleared, it proved fertile for crops like wheat, oats, and vegetables. Farmers also raised dairy cows, chickens, and pigs. Some tried apples, pears, and other fruit trees, though the wet climate sometimes caused rot and fungus. Farming families often lived modestly at first, building log cabins or small wooden houses. Over time, as they prospered, they might add a barn, a smokehouse, and a larger home.

Eastern Washington: The Drier Plateau and Irrigation

East of the Cascade Range, the climate was quite different. Rainfall was much lower, and the landscape included rolling hills, grasslands, and sagebrush plains. While the soil could be rich in many areas, farming required irrigation. Early settlers in regions like the Yakima Valley dug ditches from rivers to channel water onto their fields. This allowed them to grow wheat, hops, fruit trees, and other crops even in drier conditions.

Walla Walla became a key agricultural center, producing high-quality wheat. Farmers stored their grain in simple wooden granaries before loading it onto wagons or riverboats, then shipping it to markets. The Yakima Valley, once the system of irrigation improved, became known for producing apples, pears, and grapes. These achievements took time and effort, as well as the cooperation of neighbors to share irrigation channels. But the success stories brought more settlers each year.

Boost to Local Businesses

General Stores, Blacksmiths, and Other Services

As logging camps, canneries, and farms multiplied, they drew workers who needed tools, clothing, and household goods. Local business owners seized this opportunity by opening general stores stocked with items freighted from other parts of the country. These stores sold everything from flour and sugar to boots, nails, and fabric. Credit was sometimes offered to workers waiting for their next pay. A few store owners became community leaders, as their businesses were central meeting spots for news and conversation.

Blacksmith shops were also vital, repairing wagon wheels, forging metal parts, and shoeing horses or mules. These shops often rang with the sound of hammers on anvils. Other services included carpenters, coopers (barrel-makers), and tailors. Some adventurous souls opened small hotels or boarding houses, providing beds and meals to travelers who passed through the area.

Banking and Trading Houses

With more money changing hands in logging, fishing, and farming, small banks or trading houses began to appear in growing towns. They provided loans for bigger ventures—like building a sawmill, buying more farmland, or purchasing new machinery. These financial services were risky because the frontier economy could be unstable. Still, the need for credit drew many people into banking. Over time, a few banks expanded, helping fund roads and other improvements that supported further business development.

Social Life and Community Growth

Churches, Schools, and Gatherings

Towns and villages in Washington were not just about making money. They were places where families built a sense of community. Churches, which started small in many logging or farming areas, offered Sunday services, weddings, and baptisms. Ministers traveled between settlements, sometimes preaching in someone's home or a schoolhouse if no church building existed. Children learned to read and write in small schoolrooms, often with one teacher for all grades. The teacher might be young and untrained, but was usually committed to helping local kids learn the basics.

Music, dances, and picnics brought neighbors together. Community members might celebrate harvest time with a social gathering. Logging camps sometimes hosted "lumberjack dances," inviting women from nearby towns to come enjoy fiddles and guitars after a long workweek. Fishing communities held fish fries or salmon bakes, often sharing the day's catch with everyone. These events relieved the hard work and isolation many settlers felt.

Newspapers and Communication

Local newspapers played a big role in shaping how towns saw themselves. Papers reported on lumber yields, fishing catches, crop successes, and local politics. They also printed news of births, deaths, and weddings, helping connect people in scattered settlements. Reading material was scarce on the frontier, so a newspaper was a treasure that circulated among neighbors. Mail service was slow and sometimes irregular, but the telegraph would eventually begin to bridge these remote towns with the outside world—though that came a bit later in time.

Environmental Impact and Native Perspectives

Changing the Land and Rivers

While settlers saw progress in their growing industries, the environment felt the effects. Clear-cut logging stripped hillsides, leading to erosion. Rivers loaded with logs sometimes damaged fish habitat. In fishing, large traps and fish wheels took so many salmon that fewer returned to spawn each year. Farmers plowed grasslands for crops, which changed the landscape for animals that had grazed there for centuries.

For Native Tribes, these changes were profound. Traditional hunting, fishing, and gathering areas shrank or were heavily altered. The promise of treaty-reserved fishing rights was hard to uphold if salmon runs declined, or if settlers restricted access to riverbanks. Some tribes attempted to adapt by working in the new industries—logging, canning, or farming in European ways—but they often faced discrimination and had limited land after reservation boundaries were imposed.

Efforts to Raise Concerns

Some observers, including a few forward-thinking settlers or territorial officials, noted the potential long-term harm to forests and fish. They wrote articles or letters suggesting moderation.

However, most people were focused on making a living, and official conservation measures were nearly nonexistent in this period. It was an era of expansion and quick profit, with few regulations to limit logging or fishing.

Challenges for Workers and Families

Dangers and Low Wages

Life in these industries could be rough. Logging and fishing were among the most dangerous jobs. Falling timber, heavy saws, or boat accidents claimed many lives. Families worried every day if fathers or brothers would come home safely. Pay was also inconsistent. Workers were sometimes paid in "scrip" (credit at a company store) instead of real money. If the mill or cannery closed due to low demand or bad weather, people lost their jobs quickly.

Farmers faced their own risks. Poor weather could ruin a crop. A single drought might mean losing the entire year's harvest. Stump-filled fields were hard to plow. Pests and plant diseases showed up unexpectedly. For many, survival meant working from sunrise to sunset, relying on the help of neighbors or extended family. Yet, despite these hardships, the territory's population continued to climb, and the promise of owning land or succeeding in business drew more and more hopefuls.

Social Divisions

As towns grew, social divisions emerged. Large mill owners or wealthy merchants often held more power. Working-class loggers, fishermen, and cannery employees had fewer choices if they wanted to protest low wages or unsafe conditions. This imbalance sometimes sparked local arguments, but formal labor unions were rare in the early years. Churches and community groups tried to address social problems, offering charity to families in need. Over time, these issues would lead to more organized labor movements, but that was still in the future.

Emergence of Local Leadership

Town Councils and County Governments

With the territory forming official counties, local leadership structures arose. Towns elected mayors, sheriffs, and councils to pass ordinances—like preventing animals from roaming free in the streets or setting basic building regulations. County governments oversaw roads, schools, and law enforcement outside of towns. These leaders often had little training, but they adapted quickly, learning to manage budgets, hold public meetings, and respond to citizens' complaints.

Attempts to Coordinate Growth

Some early civic leaders recognized the need to plan for the future. They discussed where roads should go, how to attract new businesses, and how to handle disputes with local tribes. Because the territory was big and communications slow, each region handled matters somewhat differently. Puget Sound towns relied heavily on shipping, while interior areas depended on wagon roads and rivers. These local governments laid the groundwork for what would one day become state-level policies and planning.

Stepping Stones Toward Statehood

Increased Settlement and Calls for More Representation

As industries expanded, so did the population. Farmers, loggers, and fishermen wanted a stronger voice in territorial government. They needed fair laws about land claims, resource use, and taxes. People started talking more seriously about the possibility of Washington becoming a state. However, the official population had to reach certain levels before the U.S. Congress would consider granting statehood. The territory also needed a stable economy and a track record of managing its own affairs.

By the 1870s, the territory's leaders pushed harder to attract new settlers, build better roads, and strengthen local schools—all steps toward showing that Washington could handle statehood responsibilities. Industries like logging and fishing brought wealth and jobs, which in turn increased the number of permanent residents. Farming families settled entire valleys, creating stable communities that demanded better infrastructure and political clout.

Laying the Economic Foundation

Without the success of logging, fishing, and farming, Washington might have remained a remote corner of the American frontier. These industries provided the capital and stability for other ventures—like small manufacturing, shipbuilding, and trading houses—that broadened the economy. As each sector grew, it pulled the territory further into national markets. Lumber, salmon, wheat, and orchard fruits became known outside the region, establishing Washington as a land of resource wealth and potential.

CHAPTER 10

Railroads and Roads – Connecting People and Goods

Before modern highways and cars, railroads and wagon roads were the main arteries that moved people and goods across Washington. As the territory's industries—logging, fishing, and farming—boomed, the need for better transportation became urgent. Moving lumber or wheat by horse-drawn wagons was slow and expensive. Steamboats on rivers and the Puget Sound were helpful, but they did not reach inland areas easily. Railroads promised a faster, more reliable way to carry produce, logs, and travelers to distant markets.

In this chapter, we will explore the development of Washington's early rail lines and roads. We will see how investors, local leaders, and the federal government worked together—sometimes with tension, sometimes in harmony—to lay tracks across rugged landscapes. We will also look at how improved roads transformed small towns, boosted trade, and helped unify the scattered settlements of this growing territory.

Early Efforts at Better Transportation

The Problem of Distance

Washington's geography was challenging. The Cascade Range divided the state into two distinct regions: the rainy, forested west and the dry, rolling plains of the east. Towns near Puget Sound had access to water transport, but inland communities had to rely on slow wagon trails. Likewise, eastern farmers raised large wheat crops but needed reliable ways to ship them to coastal ports. As the population grew, complaints about poor roads and disconnected trade routes increased.

Leaders in each region wanted solutions but were not always sure how to pay for them. The territorial government had limited funds, and the land was vast. Some settlers hoped private companies or the federal government would invest in transportation. Others believed local taxes or bonds were the only way. Meetings were held in towns like Olympia, Vancouver, and Walla Walla, where citizens debated how to improve roads and whether rail lines could realistically be built across mountains and rivers.

Private Roads and Plank Roads

Before large-scale railroad construction began, smaller projects tried to make wagon travel less miserable. In some towns, local businessmen built toll roads—private roads for which travelers paid a fee. These might be plank roads, made of wooden boards laid across muddy areas to keep wagons from sinking. While not ideal, plank roads were an improvement, allowing farmers to haul crops year-round. However, they required constant maintenance. Rotting boards had to be replaced, and floods could wash away entire sections.

Still, these early efforts paved the way for thinking bigger. If short segments of road could help local trade, perhaps a longer, more robust system could connect entire regions of Washington. People began looking east, toward the idea of a transcontinental railroad.

The Dream of a Northern Transcontinental Railroad

Federal Land Grants

During the mid-19th century, the U.S. government passed legislation to encourage railroad building. Companies that agreed to construct rail lines received generous land grants along the proposed routes. They could sell this land to settlers or use the timber and minerals there to fund construction costs. This system helped railroads expand across the Midwest and toward the West Coast. However, deciding which route the rail line would take was a political battle—northern states pushed for a northern route, southern states for a southern route.

With the Civil War (1861–1865) in the background, the northern states gained more influence in Congress. Eventually, the idea of a northern transcontinental railroad gathered momentum. Washington leaders saw an opportunity: if the line came through the territory, it would speed up development and boost trade. But building through the rugged northern Rockies and the Cascade Range was no small feat.

Isaac Stevens and Early Surveys

In Chapter 8, we saw how Governor Isaac Stevens also served as a surveyor, exploring possible railroad routes. Stevens believed a northern line was not only possible but vital to Washington's future. His surveys in the 1850s revealed passes through the mountains—like Snoqualmie Pass and others—that might accommodate tracks. Still, winter snow and steep grades posed engineering challenges. The cost would be high, and investors worried whether enough traffic existed to justify the expense.

Nevertheless, the idea caught on. Papers in towns like Olympia and Walla Walla urged citizens to support any railroad plan that brought steel rails to their region. Local merchants imagined shipping lumber, wheat, and other goods to eastern markets. Farmers expected faster, cheaper transport that would let them compete with other states. The potential profits were huge, if only someone could lay the tracks.

Building the Northern Pacific Railroad

Founding the Company

One of the earliest and most significant rail companies to tackle Washington's terrain was the Northern Pacific Railroad (NP). Founded in 1864, it received a charter from Congress that included extensive land grants along its proposed route. The NP aimed to connect the Great Lakes region with the Puget Sound, creating a true northern coast-to-coast line. Investors came from the East Coast and Europe, tempted by the promise of owning land and profiting from shipping fees.

The company faced immediate challenges: raising enough capital, hiring skilled engineers, and dealing with harsh climates. They also had to negotiate with tribes whose lands the railroad would cross. Some tribal leaders saw economic opportunities—if stations were built, local communities might benefit. Others worried about further losses of land and disruption of hunting or fishing grounds. Treaties often did not account for rail lines, adding to the confusion.

Laying Track and Overcoming Obstacles

Construction started from multiple points. Crews laid track eastward from Kalama on the Columbia River, planning to reach Puget Sound. Another portion headed west from more eastern territories, aiming to close the gap. Workers included Civil War veterans, immigrants (especially from Ireland, Germany, and Scandinavia), and local laborers. They dug tunnels, built trestles over deep ravines, and blasted rock in remote areas.

The mountains were particularly tough. Winter storms buried work sites in snow, and avalanches threatened equipment. Workers often lived in rough camps with poorly built shacks or tents. Disease, accidents, and disputes over pay were common. Progress was slower than investors hoped, leading to financial panics when construction fell behind schedule. Newspapers followed each milestone, cheering when a bridge was completed or a tunnel was finished.

Despite these hardships, the workers pressed on, spurred by wages that—though low—were often better than what they could earn elsewhere. By the 1870s and early 1880s, key segments of the Northern Pacific took shape in Washington, linking farm regions to river ports. Eventually, the line reached across the country, and in 1883, officials drove the final "golden spike" in Montana to mark its completion. Washington was now connected to the rest of the nation by rail.

Effects of the Railroad on Washington

Boom Towns and New Settlements

Wherever the railroad stopped, settlements sprang up. Towns vied to be on the railroad's route because that meant shipping business, new residents, and economic growth. Places like Tacoma and Spokane (initially called Spokane Falls) expanded rapidly once they became major rail stops. Real estate values soared, and merchants set up shops near the depots. Hotels and restaurants accommodated travelers, while warehouses stored wheat, lumber, and other commodities waiting to be shipped.

In some areas, such as small farming communities in eastern Washington, the railroad brought a sense of hope. Farmers could now sell their wheat in distant markets without relying on slow wagon trains or uncertain river travel. In western Washington, mills sent lumber out by rail, opening up new markets in the Midwest. The territory's population climbed as more people arrived, sensing opportunities for work and land deals near the tracks.

Competition and Tensions

Not everyone welcomed the railroad with open arms. Some towns that were bypassed by the tracks suffered economic setbacks, as businesses relocated to places with better shipping options. This led to fierce lobbying and local rivalry. A community might offer free land to the railroad or promise to build a depot if the line passed through its main street.

Conflicts also arose over land grants. Farmers who settled on land granted to the railroad had to buy it at a price set by the company, which sometimes felt unfair. Others felt the railroad demanded too many privileges, such as large property holdings without immediate use. Meanwhile, tribes whose reservations were cut by rail lines found that game animals avoided the noise and activity around the tracks.

Other Rail Lines and Smaller Routes

Great Northern Railway

After the Northern Pacific, another important line appeared: the Great Northern Railway. Led by entrepreneur James J. Hill, the Great

Northern aimed to create a profitable, low-debt route from St. Paul, Minnesota, to Seattle. Completed in the 1890s, it passed through the northern parts of the Rocky Mountains and entered Washington, competing with the Northern Pacific for freight and passenger service.

Hill's approach relied less on government land grants and more on careful planning. He encouraged settlement along the route, promoting farming and town-building in areas he believed had potential. Like the Northern Pacific, the Great Northern overcame enormous geographic challenges, including deep valleys, steep grades, and harsh winter weather. Its arrival gave Washington multiple rail options, spurring even more population growth and commerce.

Short Lines and Logging Railroads

Beyond the big transcontinental lines, smaller railroads—often called "short lines"—sprang up to serve specific needs. In forested areas, logging companies built temporary rail tracks into the woods, hauling out logs on small steam locomotives known as "lokies." These rail spurs connected to main lines or rivers, ensuring a steady flow of timber to sawmills. Some short lines also served mining operations, carrying ore to smelters or docks.

Though less glamorous than the big cross-country rails, these short lines were vital to local economies. They allowed businesses to reach markets quickly, boosting jobs and wealth in remote corners of Washington. Over time, many short lines were bought by larger companies, or they closed if the resources they served were depleted.

Improvements in Roads

Territorial and County Roads

While railroads grabbed headlines, roads were still important for everyday travel, especially for those who lived away from rail lines. In the 1860s and 1870s, the territorial government encouraged counties to build and maintain roads linking farms to rail depots and towns. These roads were often simple dirt tracks, turning to mud in the rainy season and dust in summer. Bridges over rivers and creeks were wooden structures prone to flood damage.

Nevertheless, improvements slowly came. County governments used taxes or bond issues to grade roads, add gravel or planks, and put up basic signs. Stagecoaches ran on main routes, carrying mail and passengers. Farmers used these roads to bring produce to railroad stations. Even with a growing railway network, many places still depended on wagons for local transport. Good roads could save hours or days of travel time, so communities took them seriously.

Stagecoaches and Freight Lines

Stagecoach companies provided crucial connections for people who needed to visit relatives, attend court, or conduct business. They also carried the mail. Passengers often endured bumpy rides and cramped seating, but it beat walking. Freight lines used heavy-duty wagons pulled by teams of horses, mules, or oxen to move goods overland. These freight wagons hauled everything from mining equipment to barrels of flour.

While railroads offered faster shipping, not every community had a station, so roads remained vital. In fact, many railroads themselves relied on local freight wagons to bring logs or produce to the rail lines. Towns that lacked direct rail access tried to maintain the best roads possible, hoping to keep up with the booming commerce in rail-served areas.

Social and Economic Impact of Better Transportation

Easier Movement of People and Ideas

Before railroads and improved roads, communication within Washington was slow and uneven. It could take weeks to travel from the eastern wheat fields to the coastal sawmills. The new transportation systems changed that. People could visit relatives in another county, attend territorial fairs, or buy goods from different regions far more easily. Newspapers and mail traveled faster, spreading ideas, news, and political debates across the territory.

This exchange of ideas helped shape a more unified identity for Washington. As communities interacted more, they formed alliances to lobby the territorial legislature for improvements. Farmers, loggers, fishers, and merchants shared concerns about taxes, land rights, and other issues. The territory, once a patchwork of isolated settlements, took on a stronger, collective voice.

Growth of Towns into Cities

Railroads had a dramatic effect on specific towns. Seattle and Tacoma both vied to become the main terminus on Puget Sound for the Northern Pacific. Tacoma ultimately won the official designation for that line, leading to a population surge. Meanwhile, Seattle found other ways to attract investors and secured later lines, eventually outgrowing its rival. Spokane, strategically located near farming and mining regions, grew rapidly once the railroad arrived there, becoming a major commercial center in eastern Washington.

These evolving towns built more advanced infrastructure, including brick buildings, electric streetlights (when that technology became available later in the century), and water systems. Banks, hotels, and schools all expanded. Immigrants from Europe and elsewhere in the United States arrived, drawn by jobs in railroad construction, sawmills, fishing canneries, and farmland. The territory became more diverse and more economically complex.

Challenges and Controversies

Corporate Power and Land Disputes

As rail companies gained wealth and influence, some settlers began to resent them. They felt railroad corporations charged high freight rates, profited from land grants, and influenced local politics. Farmers who needed to ship wheat or fruit had little choice but to pay whatever the railroad demanded. Land disputes, where the railroad claimed ownership over properties already occupied by homesteaders, led to lawsuits and anger.

Various farmer organizations arose—sometimes called "granges"—to fight for fair shipping rates and to push politicians to regulate railroads. Although these groups gained strength later, the seeds of such movements took hold in this period of rapid railroad expansion. People realized that while rail lines were vital to growth, unchecked corporate power could harm small businesses and individual settlers.

Environmental and Cultural Impacts

As with logging, fishing, and farming, the expansion of railroads and roads further changed the environment. Tunnels and trestles altered natural landscapes. Noise and human activity pushed wildlife away from travel corridors. Native Tribes found their lands further fragmented, and access to traditional hunting or fishing sites became even more limited if tracks or roads blocked migration routes or cut through reservations.

The cultural shift was also significant. Some tribal communities adapted by trading at rail stations or running small businesses serving travelers. Others felt even more marginalized. While a few treaties included provisions for crossing tribal lands, many did not anticipate the scale or speed of development, leaving tribes to cope with broken agreements and sudden changes in land use.

Pushing Toward Statehood

Increased Unity

The new transportation links helped unify the territory, making it easier for delegates to gather in the capital to discuss statehood. Leaders from different corners of Washington could now travel by train (or a combination of rail and roads) to settle legislative matters. The once-isolated eastern farms, coastal cities, and southwestern logging communities now shared more economic interests and better communication.

This unity was crucial. If Washington wanted to become a state, it needed to present itself as a coherent region capable of self-government, with stable industries and the infrastructure to support continued growth. The railroads, in particular, served as a visible sign of progress—an indication that Washington could play a major role in the nation's future.

Meeting Population and Development Requirements

Congress had certain requirements before admitting new states. Washington needed a large enough population, functioning institutions, and a track record of resolving major issues. By the late 1880s, the territory had seen enough growth—fueled largely by rail and road improvements—that it met or exceeded these benchmarks. Towns were thriving, agriculture was booming, and the lumber and fishing industries continued to expand.

Although formal statehood came in 1889, well beyond the immediate scope of this chapter, the transportation developments of the 1870s and 1880s laid much of the groundwork. Without railroads and decent roads, Washington would have struggled to move goods to market, attract new residents, or develop a unifying identity. The territory's future hinged on these connections, and the people of Washington worked hard to make them a reality.

The Human Stories of Travel

Railroad Workers and Road Builders

Behind each stretch of track or mile of road were the hands of real people. Railroad crews worked in dangerous conditions—blasting rock in tunnels, laying ties in swamps, or bridging deep gorges. Many were recent immigrants who spoke little English. Road builders, often hired by county governments, spent long days grading and laying gravel. Others built wooden bridges that washed out in the next flood, forcing them to start over.

Despite low pay, the sense of accomplishment was strong. Workers could look back at finished rail segments or newly passable roads with pride, knowing they had tamed a piece of wild land. Some kept diaries or letters describing the struggles of high mountain passes, the beauty of remote forests, and the relief of reaching a supply station after weeks in the wilderness.

Travelers' Experiences

For settlers traveling by rail for the first time, the ride could feel like a miracle. A trip that once took weeks by wagon might take only days by train. Passengers marveled at the changing landscapes flying by their windows. Stagecoach travelers on improved roads still faced bumps, dust, or mud, but the existence of reliable bridges and rest stops made the journey far safer than before.

Families sometimes moved across the country on these new lines, bringing all their possessions in freight cars. They stepped off into a Washington that was still rough around the edges, but full of promise. Hotels near depots bustled with newcomers asking for directions to local land offices or inquiring about job openings in logging camps, sawmills, or canneries.

Looking Ahead

As we have seen, the arrival of railroads and the improvement of roads brought profound changes to Washington. The territory's economy expanded, towns grew into cities, and people could travel more easily than ever before. Yet these developments also sparked controversies over land, corporate power, and environmental damage. Native Tribes faced more challenges, and not all communities benefited equally from the new infrastructure.

In the upcoming chapters, we will continue to follow the path of Washington's growth. We will see how it transitioned into statehood and explore the daily life of its early inhabitants—families, workers, and community leaders—who shaped the culture of the region. The foundation laid by railways and roads would remain vital in connecting people, ideas, and goods, proving that a once-isolated frontier was rapidly joining the mainstream of American life.

CHAPTER 11

The Making of a State – Washington Joins the Union

By the late 1800s, Washington Territory had changed greatly from its early frontier days. Towns were growing, industries were expanding, and railroads connected people from coast to coast. Many residents felt their region had outgrown its territorial status. They wanted full rights and representation under the U.S. Constitution. They believed it was time for Washington to become a state.

In this chapter, we will see how Washington took the final steps toward statehood. We will learn about the political campaigns, the drafting of a constitution, and the challenges that slowed the process. We will also explore how statehood changed life for residents, and how it created new responsibilities for the leaders they elected.

The Road to Statehood

Early Attempts and Delays

Washington officially became a territory in 1853. From that time forward, some citizens and leaders talked about eventual statehood. However, the territory's population was small in the 1850s and 1860s, and the Civil War (1861–1865) took national attention away from western issues. Even after the war, Congress had many other matters to handle, so admitting new states was not always a top priority.

Additionally, the federal government needed assurance that new states had stable economies, functional governments, and enough people. By the 1870s, Washington was growing faster, thanks to logging, fishing, farming, and an increasing number of rail lines. As more families settled, the territory built schools, improved roads, and expanded commerce. Still, some in Congress believed Washington was not quite ready.

Population Growth and Economic Progress

Throughout the 1880s, the population soared. Towns like Seattle, Tacoma, Spokane, and Walla Walla saw waves of newcomers from other U.S. states and from abroad. Real estate boomed. Lumber mills sent their products far and wide. Wheat farmers exported grain on newly built railroads. Fishing canneries lined coastal regions and riverbanks. These industries provided jobs and a flow of money, convincing more leaders that Washington could handle statehood.

In 1883, the Northern Pacific Railroad completed its line through Stampede Pass in the Cascade Mountains, further linking eastern and western Washington. Soon the Great Northern Railroad followed. Travelers noticed busy ports, thriving towns, and a sense of optimism. By 1887, census data suggested that Washington's population was well above the threshold needed for statehood, though official counts were not always exact. Local politicians and newspapers pressed harder for the territory's admission as a state.

The Enabling Act of 1889

Congressional Approval

To become a state, Washington needed an act of Congress—often called an "enabling act"—that authorized its people to frame a state constitution and government. In 1889, Congress passed an act that grouped Washington together with Montana and the Dakotas, all of which were on the path to statehood. This law allowed these territories to hold constitutional conventions, where elected delegates would draft constitutions outlining how their new state governments would function.

For Washington, the enabling act was a major milestone. It signaled that Congress believed the territory was ready to govern itself more fully. It also meant that Washington's citizens would soon vote on whether to accept their proposed constitution. Once that vote happened, and if the constitution met Congress's conditions, President Benjamin Harrison could sign the official proclamation admitting Washington as a state.

The Constitutional Convention

Delegates for Washington's constitutional convention were elected from various districts in the territory. These men (women were not yet allowed to serve in such roles) gathered in Olympia, the territorial capital, in July 1889. Their task was to write a document that explained the powers of the state government, the rights of citizens, and the structure of the legislature, courts, and executive offices.

Over the summer, they debated important topics:

- **Legislative Representation**: How many members should each county have?
- **Governor's Powers**: Should the governor have the right to veto laws passed by the legislature?
- **Taxation and Public Debt**: How could the new state raise money without burdening citizens too heavily?
- **Rights of Women and Minorities**: Although the final constitution did not grant women the right to vote (that would come later), some delegates argued for greater inclusion.

- **Education**: The delegates wanted to protect public schools and outline a system for funding them.

After weeks of debate, they produced a constitution that reflected the values of many Washington residents: a focus on education, an independent judiciary, and a balance of powers among the branches of government. Even though not everyone agreed on every detail, most delegates believed this constitution would serve the new state well.

Ratification and Statehood

Voting on the Constitution

Once the convention ended, the proposed constitution was printed and shared with citizens across Washington Territory. Newspapers ran articles explaining its main points, while local leaders gave speeches urging people to approve (or reject) certain provisions. Voters then cast ballots in October 1889 to say "yes" or "no" to this new constitution. The majority voted in favor. Washington's leaders quickly forwarded the results to President Benjamin Harrison, along with copies of the constitution and other official documents.

The Official Proclamation

On November 11, 1889, President Harrison signed the proclamation admitting Washington to the Union as the 42nd state. Crowds in Olympia, Seattle, Tacoma, Spokane, and many smaller towns celebrated. Church bells rang, cannons boomed, and parades filled the streets. Businesses flew flags, while newspapers announced the news in bold headlines. After decades of territorial status, Washington finally had equal standing with the older states. Its citizens gained full rights, including the ability to elect representatives and senators to the U.S. Congress.

Statehood also brought new responsibilities. The territory's governor became the first state governor, Elisha P. Ferry, who had been elected under the new constitution's rules. The legislature had broader powers to pass laws, collect taxes, and manage state lands. Courts expanded to handle not just territorial cases but also those under the state's jurisdiction.

Shifting Political Landscape

Formation of State Institutions

With Washington's entry into the Union, state institutions took shape. The state legislature—divided into a Senate and House of Representatives—began enacting laws on topics from public schools to road building. A state supreme court formed, hearing appeals and clarifying how state laws should be interpreted. These institutions worked out of existing buildings in Olympia, though they would eventually need larger, more permanent structures.

Local governments also adjusted. Counties gained certain rights under the state constitution, such as the ability to pass local regulations or levy taxes for roads and public works. Cities could incorporate under state law, forming city councils and hiring police chiefs. In effect, statehood brought a new level of structure and complexity to government functions, making them more responsive to local needs.

Political Parties and Voter Participation

Before statehood, territorial politics were often influenced by a few powerful personalities. Now, major national parties like the Republicans and Democrats established firmer bases in Washington. They held conventions, nominated candidates, and campaigned more vigorously for votes. Newspapers aligned themselves with one party or the other, printing editorials to sway public opinion.

Voter participation rose as well, although women, Native Americans (not considered full citizens at the time), and many immigrants without naturalization status still could not vote. Still, the pool of eligible voters grew, and elections began to carry more weight. Debates took place on how to shape the state's future: Should it focus on farming or lumber, or both? Should it encourage foreign investment in railroads and mines? Which social reforms deserved attention?

Impact on Everyday Life

More Influence in National Affairs

As a state, Washington could now send two senators and a representative (later more, as population grew) to the U.S. Congress. This meant that issues important to Washington—such as federal funding for harbor improvements, irrigation projects, or Indian

Affairs—might get more attention. Citizens who once felt overshadowed by larger states in the West now had direct voices in national politics.

Education and Public Lands

Statehood also allowed Washington to benefit from federal land grants for schools and other public purposes. The state constitution set aside sections of land in each township to support public education, leading to the creation of school districts across the region. Universities and colleges, such as the University of Washington (which had started earlier as a territorial institution), gained more stable funding from state authorities.

Additionally, the new state could manage its own public lands and possibly earn revenue from leasing or selling them. That income might fund roads, bridges, schools, and other improvements. While the federal government still oversaw large areas of forest and reserves, Washington had greater control over its destiny in managing resources—although that control was not total and remained limited by federal laws in some cases.

Challenges After Statehood

Economic Booms and Busts

Even as Washington celebrated statehood, it faced economic ups and downs. Real estate speculation had driven land prices high in the late 1880s, and when demand cooled, some investors went bankrupt. Logging, fishing, and farming still formed the backbone of the economy, but they depended on resource availability and market prices. Overfishing or poor logging practices sometimes caused short-term slumps, leading to unemployment.

Nevertheless, many entrepreneurs remained optimistic. After all, the territory's new rail links and official state status seemed certain to draw more settlers and businesses. People opened banks, formed companies, and built steam-powered mills, confident that Washington's resources would continue to attract customers from other parts of the nation.

Conflicts with Native Tribes

Becoming a state did not resolve longstanding tensions with Native Tribes, who had lost large portions of land to treaties and settlement. Many tribal members questioned whether the new state government would honor treaty rights—especially regarding fishing, hunting, and reservation boundaries. The federal government still officially handled most Indian Affairs, but state policies, such as laws about fish runs or land usage, often impacted tribal livelihoods. Some tribes tried to work with the new state leaders; others resisted or took their disputes to federal courts.

Over time, disagreements about land, water, or resource use sometimes flared into legal or political battles. Native communities struggled to maintain their cultures and economies under state and federal systems that did not fully respect their sovereignty. Statehood, in many cases, meant that non-Native lawmakers could pass regulations affecting land or waters that tribes had depended on for generations.

Women's Rights and Other Reforms

Although women did not gain the right to vote in Washington's 1889 constitution, they continued to push for suffrage. Various women's clubs, churches, and community groups organized gatherings and petition drives. They argued that women had proven essential to frontier life and should have a say in shaping the state's future. Other reform movements also arose, like those aiming to limit alcohol sales or improve labor conditions. The new state government had to grapple with calls for social changes that had not always been heard during the territorial period.

Cities on the Rise

Seattle, Tacoma, and Spokane

Statehood gave a further boost to Washington's major cities. Seattle benefited from shipping routes, a developing railroad network, and its deep-water port. Tacoma, chosen by the Northern Pacific as its western terminus, attracted mills and factories along Commencement Bay. Spokane, connected to farming and mining regions in the east, grew into a bustling commercial center. These cities built brick and stone buildings downtown, installed streetcar systems (in the 1890s), and formed fire departments to protect against frequent blazes in wooden structures.

In the aftermath of Washington's admission to the Union, city leaders wanted to show that they belonged among the important urban centers of the West. They organized fairs and exhibitions, inviting visitors from across the country. Hotels rose to accommodate travelers, and newspapers boasted of business opportunities. Though Seattle, Tacoma, and Spokane sometimes competed fiercely, they also recognized their roles in the larger statewide economy.

Smaller Towns and Regional Hubs

Beyond the major cities, smaller towns also felt the effects of statehood. Communities like Walla Walla, Yakima, Ellensburg, and Bellingham expanded their local industries, welcomed more settlers, and improved their public services. Town councils worked with county and state officials on matters like road improvements and school funding. Being part of a state (rather than a territory) often made it easier to get outside investment, such as loans for building sawmills, canneries, or fruit-packing facilities. Farmers around these towns found new markets for their goods and, in some cases, formed cooperatives to share equipment or storage.

Cultural Life and Identity

Newspapers, Clubs, and Social Organizations

With statehood, Washington took on a more robust cultural identity. Dozens of newspapers circulated, informing readers about local happenings and national events. Editorials discussed the new state's future, including how to attract industries and immigrants. Social clubs—like Masonic lodges, reading circles, and charitable groups—multiplied. Church groups organized socials, picnics, and fundraisers. School events, such as spelling bees or musical recitals, drew families together, fostering a sense of pride in community achievements.

Some residents wanted to showcase Washington's natural beauty, from Mount Rainier to the Pacific coastline. They wrote articles praising the region's mild climate, lush forests, and productive farmland. Brochures and pamphlets were sent to the eastern states, luring more settlers with promises of a bright future in the new state. Although life could still be hard on farms or in logging camps, the overall tone was one of hope.

Art, Music, and Local Traditions

While Washington did not yet have large theaters or concert halls in every city, local musicians, traveling performers, and theater troupes visited towns and staged shows. Folk dances and community singing were common at gatherings. Some artists painted or sketched the dramatic landscapes, while local photographers captured images of logging sites, city streets, and newly built schools. These works of art gave people back east a glimpse of what Washington looked like, beyond the written descriptions.

Local traditions also combined with older Native practices, though the latter often remained outside mainstream acceptance. Nevertheless, some non-Native citizens grew curious about Native arts, crafts, and stories, seeing them as part of the state's heritage. Few official efforts were made to preserve tribal culture at this time, however. Most attention stayed on the "modern" aspects of the new state's growth.

The Role of Federal and State Lands

Forests, Mines, and Irrigation

Upon achieving statehood, Washington gained certain public lands from the federal government, particularly for schools and public institutions. Yet the federal government still owned large portions of forested and mountainous areas. As logging companies pushed deeper into the woods, there were calls for better management to avoid depleting the forests entirely. Some state leaders supported the idea of forest reserves, though official conservation policies remained weak until later.

In mineral-rich parts of Washington, mines produced coal, gold, silver, and other metals. State officials tried to regulate safety conditions, but enforcement was often uneven. Irrigation projects also expanded in places like the Yakima and Wenatchee Valleys, where farmers wanted to turn arid land into productive orchards. Statehood made it somewhat easier to coordinate such projects, as the new government could work with local irrigation districts and private investors.

Balancing Growth and Preservation

As the new state forged ahead, few laws controlled how forests or fisheries should be managed for future generations. While some voices called for limiting the catch of salmon or setting aside forest land, business interests favored rapid exploitation for profit. Even those who worried about depletion found it hard to pass protective legislation against powerful logging or fishing companies. Thus, while statehood brought more local control, it did not guarantee wise stewardship of natural resources. That debate would unfold in the years to come.

Legacy of Statehood

A Step into National Politics

With two new senators and a representative in the U.S. House, Washington's voice in national policy grew. Over time, this would influence federal spending on harbor improvements, agricultural research stations, and other projects that benefited the state's economy. It also put Washington on the political map, with elected officials who joined national debates on tariffs, labor laws, and other issues.

Pride and Responsibility

Statehood gave Washington residents a sense of pride. They were no longer just "territorial citizens" but full members of the United States, with constitutional guarantees and the right to help shape the nation's future. This also brought responsibility—Washington lawmakers had to manage budgets, care for roads, build schools, and ensure fair treatment under the law. Although not everyone enjoyed equal rights, the new constitution did lay down principles of governance that affected all inhabitants, whether settlers or Native peoples (the latter, sadly, were often overlooked in practice).

Future developments—like the women's suffrage movement, labor movements, and the push for conservation—would arise from the foundation laid in 1889. The immediate years after statehood were full of possibility and also challenges. Conflicts over natural resources, minority rights, and fair economic growth were far from settled. Yet, Washington had taken a big step toward determining its own path within the American family of states.

Looking Ahead

As we have seen, the making of a state was not a simple or quick process. Many forces—economic, political, and social—came together in the 1880s to push Washington over the threshold of statehood. Achieving it brought celebrations, new institutions, and a stronger voice in national affairs. It also opened the door to fresh debates about how best to govern, share resources, and include all citizens in the promise of a better life.

In the next chapter, we will look closer at daily life in early Washington—how families, schools, and towns operated during this time of change. We will see what it meant to settle in a young state still marked by frontier conditions, where roads were rough, jobs were tough, and yet optimism often flourished. This everyday perspective will help us understand the human side of Washington's journey from a raw territory to a place that many proudly called home.

CHAPTER 12

Daily Life in Early Washington – Families, Schools, and Towns

While political events and economic growth shaped Washington's larger story, everyday life for most residents revolved around homes, neighborhoods, and local communities. After statehood in 1889, the region still had a strong frontier spirit—roads were often rough, towns were small compared to eastern U.S. cities, and people needed to rely on each other for help and companionship. In this chapter, we will explore the day-to-day experiences of families, schools, and towns during Washington's formative years as a new state.

We will look at how families built and furnished their homes, the types of chores and jobs they did, and the ways they found entertainment. We will also examine what education looked like in early schools, how teachers worked with limited resources, and how communities valued learning. Lastly, we will peek into the social life of towns—markets, fairs, local organizations, and the religious institutions that played key roles in bringing people together.

Homesteads and Town Homes

Building a House

Many early Washington families lived on homesteads, especially in rural areas. They cleared land, cut logs, and built simple log cabins or rough-sawn wooden houses. In forested regions, it was easy to find building materials but hard work to clear the land. Large stumps could remain in fields for years until they could be blasted or dug out. In drier eastern parts of the state, settlers sometimes built timber-frame houses if they could afford to buy and transport lumber. Others lived in sod structures—though these were more common on the Great Plains to the east—until they had the means for something sturdier.

Flooring might be packed dirt in very humble homes or rough-hewn planks in places with easier access to mills. Windows were precious; some homes used greased paper or fabric before acquiring real glass. Roofs were typically covered with wooden shingles, which needed occasional replacement. A single fireplace or a cast-iron stove provided heat, cooked meals, and sometimes doubled as a place to keep water warm for washing.

Furnishings and Daily Tasks

A typical frontier home had few furnishings: a table, chairs (often homemade), and beds or bunks. In the kitchen area, pots, pans, and utensils hung from hooks or nails. The family might have one cupboard for dishes, which could be tin plates, cups, and a few ceramic items if they were lucky. A cradle for a baby or a small rocking chair for an elderly family member might be among the limited comforts.

Families carried water from a spring or a nearby creek. Children often helped with chores like fetching water, collecting firewood, or feeding chickens. Laundry was done by hand, scrubbing clothes on a washboard. Long winter evenings might be spent around a lantern or candle, mending clothes or reading a Bible or newspaper if available. For many, life was a cycle of chores tied to the land and the seasons—planting, harvesting, preserving food, and preparing for the next round of labor.

Work and Occupations

Farming and Ranching

Farming was a central occupation, especially east of the Cascade Range where wide expanses of land allowed for larger-scale grain production. Wheat was a major crop, along with oats, barley, and, in some irrigated areas, fruit orchards. Families kept a few cows for milk and butter, and goats or sheep for wool if they had enough space. Chickens provided eggs and meat. In heavily forested western Washington, some farmers cleared small plots among the trees, growing vegetables and tending livestock.

Ranching took hold in grassland areas, where settlers grazed cattle, sheep, or horses. Ranchers often built simple barns or corrals with split rails. They rode out daily to check on the herds, protect them from predators, and move them to fresh grazing land. As local markets grew—especially with rail connections—farmers and ranchers had new opportunities to sell their products to logging camps, mines, or growing cities.

Logging, Mining, and Fishing

For those not on farms, resource industries provided work:

- **Logging**: Men labored in logging camps or at sawmills, felling trees and processing lumber. Others built and ran small logging rail lines, hauling logs to larger mills.
- **Mining**: Some areas had deposits of coal, gold, silver, or other metals. Prospectors and miners set up small camps, living in tents or rough shacks. Life was uncertain, with booms and busts common.
- **Fishing**: Along rivers and the coast, fishing and canning were major employers. Crews netted salmon, halibut, or cod, while cannery workers processed fish for sale. Seasonal work could be grueling, but it paid better than some farm labor jobs.

Women often worked at home or in domestic service, though some ran boarding houses, did laundry for loggers or miners, or helped with local shops. A few women taught school or served as nurses. Children pitched in with chores from a young age, learning skills that would one day help them support a household or farm of their own.

Schooling and Education

One-Room Schoolhouses

In many areas of early Washington, schools were basic, one-room buildings made of logs or simple boards. One teacher taught all grades, often using whatever books were on hand. Subjects focused on reading, writing, arithmetic, spelling, and geography. Older students helped younger ones when the teacher was busy with another group. Chalkboards, if available, were precious resources. Pupils used slates to practice writing and arithmetic, since paper was scarce and expensive.

School sessions were sometimes shorter than in modern times. Children were needed at home for planting or harvest, so they might attend only part of the year. Families contributed firewood to heat the schoolhouse, and mothers took turns sending homemade lunches for children who traveled far. Discipline could be strict; teachers were expected to keep order, and misbehaving students might receive corporal punishment like a rap on the knuckles with a ruler.

Teachers and Their Challenges

Teachers were often young and single, living in boarding houses or with local families. Their salaries were low, and they handled many responsibilities—planning lessons, keeping attendance records, and maintaining the schoolhouse. Some teachers took great pride in improving literacy rates, encouraging older students to aim for advanced education or teacher training themselves.

Communities valued education as a path to success. Even if families had little cash, they donated time, goods, or labor to keep the school running. Over time, once Washington achieved statehood, public education gained more support. County or state funds helped pay teachers and build slightly better facilities. High schools began appearing in larger towns, though it took years before secondary education became common in rural areas.

Town Life and Community Bonds

Main Streets and Businesses

In larger towns, wooden sidewalks and dirt streets lined rows of shops: general stores, blacksmiths, bakeries, and saloons. Hotels and boarding houses catered to travelers, workers, and salespeople. A local newspaper might operate in a small building with a hand-cranked press. Banks offered loans and held deposits, though not every town had one. Many businesses had false fronts—tall wooden facades that made the building look more impressive from the street.

Social life flourished on the main street. People ran errands, greeted neighbors, and shared news. Farmers from the outskirts came to town on Saturdays to sell produce or buy supplies. Women browsed dry goods stores for fabric, thread, and household items. Children ran along the boardwalk, gazing in shop windows. Horses stood tied outside, occasionally spooked by steam engines or dogs.

The town might also have a community hall or meeting place for gatherings, dances, or public lectures. Some had a volunteer fire department, using a hand-pulled hose cart or a simple wagon with water barrels. Street lighting was minimal, often just kerosene lamps or early electric lights if the town had installed generators (this was more common closer to 1900).

Churches and Social Clubs

Churches played a major role in shaping community life. Congregations gathered on Sundays, then again during the week for prayer meetings, potluck suppers, or choir practice. Ministers sometimes traveled between multiple towns, holding services on different days. Church events offered a break from daily work, allowing neighbors to build strong social ties.

Various clubs, like literary societies or temperance groups, also united people around shared interests. Women formed sewing circles to make quilts for fundraisers or help widows in need. Men's lodges, such as the Masons or Odd Fellows, sponsored charitable activities and gave members a place to socialize. These institutions were often the backbone of civic life, stepping in to help in times of illness, fire, or other hardships.

Leisure, Celebrations, and Entertainment

Music, Dances, and Picnics

Even though life involved hard work, early Washington settlers found ways to relax and celebrate. Music was a favorite pastime. Families sang around the fireplace, or small groups formed string bands with fiddles, banjos, and guitars. Dance halls hosted Saturday night gatherings, where neighbors square danced, waltzed, or reeled to lively tunes. These dances could last late into the night, offering a joyful release from daily routines.

Picnics were common in the warmer months, often tied to national holidays like the Fourth of July. People brought baskets of food—fried chicken, pies, fresh fruit, cornbread—and children played games such as tag or sack races. Sometimes church groups organized these events, mixing worship and fellowship with shared meals and conversation. County fairs and harvest festivals showcased prized livestock, homemade crafts, and produce competitions. Winners displayed blue ribbons, and the fairs fostered pride in the region's agricultural bounty.

Traveling Shows and Newspapers

Traveling performers, circuses, and medicine shows occasionally toured small towns. They set up tents on vacant lots, entertaining crowds with music, juggling, or novelty acts. Medicine shows sold miracle cures and tonics, often with dubious claims. While some locals viewed these shows with skepticism, others enjoyed the rare spectacle.

Reading material included newspapers, almanacs, and the occasional novel. Newspapers, circulated widely, covered local events and gossip, plus snippets of national or world news. "Penny dreadfuls" or dime novels offered adventurous stories for those who could afford them. Families sometimes treasured a small home library of a few classic books, passed down through generations, or donated by traveling missionaries.

Health, Medicine, and Challenges

Home Remedies and Frontier Doctors

In this era, healthcare was basic. Many families relied on home remedies—teas, poultices, and folk medicine—to treat illnesses or minor injuries. Frontier doctors traveled by horseback or buggy, carrying bags of medicines. They handled everything from broken bones to childbirth. Surgical knowledge was limited, and anesthesia was still rudimentary, often just chloroform or ether if available.

Women often served as midwives, assisting with childbirth among friends and neighbors. Herbal knowledge was passed down through families, and some communities had "granny women" known for their healing skills. As towns grew, a few established small clinics or hospitals, but these were rare outside major centers. Diseases like tuberculosis, diphtheria, and typhoid fever could spread quickly, and vaccinations were limited.

Harsh Weather and Natural Disasters

Both eastern and western Washington faced challenging weather at times. On the coast and in the Puget Sound area, heavy rains might flood roads or fields. Fierce storms occasionally battered coastal towns, damaging fishing boats and docks. In the east, scorching summers, dust storms, and harsh winters tested farmers and ranchers. Snow could trap families in their homes for days, cutting off supplies.

Wildfires in timber country threatened logging camps and settlements. A single spark from a steam locomotive or a careless campfire could ignite thousands of acres of forest. Early firefighting tools were simple—buckets, axes, and shovels. The Great Seattle Fire of 1889 (the same year Washington became a state) destroyed much of the city's downtown, illustrating how quickly a blaze could level wooden structures. Towns rebuilt, often with brick and stone, learning from hard experience.

Diversity in Communities

Immigrants and Cultural Traditions

Washington's early population included immigrants from many countries. Scandinavian settlers found work in logging or fishing, bringing traditions such as Christmas celebrations with special foods and dances. Germans, Irish, Italians, and others formed neighborhoods in emerging cities, opening ethnic restaurants or social clubs. Chinese immigrants worked in canneries, on railroads, or in laundries. While they faced discrimination and legal barriers, they contributed greatly to local economies.

This mixture of cultures made some towns lively melting pots of languages, customs, and religious practices. However, prejudice and unfair laws also appeared. Some communities tried to exclude Chinese workers, and land ownership for non-white settlers was often restricted by unwritten or written rules. Native Tribes, with histories going back thousands of years, lived mostly on reservations or in segregated areas, forced to adapt to a rapidly changing world.

Women's Roles and Efforts for Change

Despite being excluded from voting in the early statehood years, women took on leadership in clubs, churches, and charitable organizations. They organized fundraising for schools or libraries, taught Sunday school, and sometimes wrote columns in local newspapers. Over time, the women's suffrage movement gained support, though it would take until 1910 for Washington women to achieve the right to vote.

Some women owned businesses or farms if they were widowed or single, proving resourceful in a society that often saw them only as wives and mothers. Slowly, their roles expanded in teaching, nursing, and other fields. Even so, traditional expectations remained strong, and daily tasks like cooking, cleaning, and child-rearing could be demanding without modern conveniences.

The Spirit of Community

Neighborly Cooperation

Life in early Washington demanded cooperation. Neighbors pitched in for barn-raisings, harvest help, or road repairs. When a family fell ill, others delivered food or took care of the livestock. During births or deaths, the community offered support. In mining or logging camps, workers often pooled resources to help an injured colleague, or to raise money for a family in need.

Small-town newspapers ran announcements of church events, weddings, funerals, and barn dances. Local leaders—like a town's mayor, a school principal, or a well-respected doctor—helped resolve disputes. This informal network of mutual aid and moral guidance created a bond that helped communities survive hardships and celebrate successes together.

Law and Order

Sheriffs and constables enforced basic laws, but in remote areas, law enforcement was spread thin. People often handled minor disputes themselves, relying on local elders or community mediation. Serious crimes like theft, horse rustling, or violence stirred up strong reactions, and vigilante actions sometimes occurred. Over time, as the state government grew, more formal courts and police departments emerged, bringing a more structured legal system to towns and counties.

Looking Toward the Future

By the early 1890s, Washington was still a young state with a frontier lifestyle, but it was growing steadily. Industries and transportation networks continued to expand, drawing more settlers each year. Families who had arrived decades earlier now saw a new generation inheriting their lands and businesses. Schools improved, and some towns built larger brick or stone public buildings, hinting at future urban development.

Life remained far from easy. Diseases, economic swings, and environmental hazards posed constant challenges. Yet many

Washington residents held an optimistic view. They believed the region's abundant timber, fish, and farmland would support continued prosperity. The spirit of cooperation, curiosity, and determination that marked daily life in these early years helped shape the state's culture for decades to come.

Conclusion and Transition

This chapter offered a glimpse into the lives of everyday people in early Washington—families building homes, children going to one-room schools, and neighbors joining together to solve problems. It showed how small towns organized, how local traditions thrived, and how women and men adapted to the state's new structure after 1889.

In the next chapters, we will continue our journey, looking at key moments and developments in Washington's early 1900s. We will explore how the region faced more rapid changes in technology, labor movements, and social life. But before we move forward, we can remember that much of modern Washington's identity grew from these humble, hardworking days—where simple wood-frame houses, smoky sawmills, and neighborly bonds formed the core of community life.

CHAPTER 13

Native Resistance and Treaties – Battles and Agreements

By the mid-1800s, conflicts between Native Tribes and newcomers in Washington had intensified. Earlier chapters described how missionaries, fur traders, and settlers disrupted traditional ways of life, pushed Native communities off their lands, and spread diseases. In response, some tribes formed alliances, resisted treaty terms they considered unfair, or fought back when they felt threatened. In this chapter, we will take a closer look at the process of treaty-making and the battles that arose when treaties were broken or misunderstood. We will learn about key tribes and leaders, the role of figures like Governor Isaac Stevens, and the long-lasting effects these agreements and conflicts had on both Native peoples and the new settlers.

Treaty-Making in a Changing Land

The U.S. Government's Goals

From the viewpoint of the federal government, treaties were supposed to define specific areas of land for tribes and open the rest for settlement by American pioneers. Officials believed that if tribes settled on reservations, conflicts could be reduced. Reservation boundaries would be set, annual payments (annuities) would be promised, and the government would introduce farming or other forms of subsistence as a new way of life. In reality, many of these promises were either broken, delayed, or never fully funded. Settlers continued to move onto tribal lands, ignoring boundaries and inflaming tensions.

In Washington, Governor Isaac Stevens also served as the Superintendent of Indian Affairs. He traveled around the territory in the 1850s to hold treaty councils with various tribes. Stevens aimed to quickly secure land for settlers and plan for roads and railroads. His tight schedule often left little time for real dialogue with tribal leaders, and translators might not convey everything accurately. This led to confusion about what was being agreed upon.

Tribal Reactions and Concerns

Tribes across the region had their own views. They saw how rapidly settlers were arriving, how game was disappearing, and how diseases were harming their populations. Some leaders believed that signing treaties might protect at least a portion of their ancestral lands and preserve their fishing or hunting rights. Others distrusted the government's words, pointing out earlier broken promises.

Even in the same tribe, opinions could vary. Some leaders wanted to find a peaceful solution to avoid the destruction of their people, while others preferred active resistance. Small groups sometimes tried to fight or raid settlements, hoping to discourage further encroachment. This diversity of responses often puzzled settlers, who thought of tribes as single units with a single voice—an assumption that was far from true.

Important Treaties and Their Terms

Medicine Creek Treaty (1854)

One early agreement was the Medicine Creek Treaty, signed in 1854. Governor Stevens met with representatives of the Nisqually, Puyallup, and other smaller tribes in a forested area near what is now Olympia. Under this treaty, tribes ceded millions of acres to the United States and, in return, were granted small reservations. They were also promised the right to fish in their "usual and accustomed" places, a clause that would become important for future legal battles.

However, the reservations assigned were often tiny compared to the tribes' original homelands. For the Nisqually people, the land set aside was far from the Nisqually River, making it hard to continue their traditional fishing. Chief Leschi of the Nisqually strongly opposed the treaty terms, believing they would destroy his people's way of life. This set the stage for conflict.

Point Elliott Treaty (1855)

The Point Elliott Treaty involved Governor Stevens and representatives of the Duwamish, Suquamish, and other coastal tribes around Puget Sound. Signed near present-day Mukilteo, it ceded even more land. Tribes were again promised small reservations, annuities, and access to fishing grounds. Chiefs like Seattle (for whom the city of Seattle is named) signed, hoping to preserve peace.

However, tribal members soon realized the government might not fulfill its promises. As settlers poured into Puget Sound, they restricted Native fishing areas, cut down forests, and built structures that blocked traditional canoe routes. While some tribal members adapted by working for settlers or trading fish and goods, others resented losing access to the best resources.

Walla Walla Council (1855)

One of the largest and most significant gatherings took place at Walla Walla in southeastern Washington. Stevens met with multiple tribes, including the Yakama, Walla Walla, Cayuse, and Umatilla. The resulting treaties carved out reservations like the Yakama Reservation, ceding millions of acres of land to the United States. Chief Kamiakin of the Yakama was among those who questioned these terms, worried that the promised goods and services would never truly materialize.

Once again, confusion about boundaries and annual payments led to mistrust. Settlers and miners continued entering tribal lands, especially after gold was discovered, and few officials seemed willing to enforce reservation boundaries. Tension exploded into open fighting not long after these treaties were signed.

Key Conflicts and Battles

The Cayuse War (1847–1855) Revisited

We touched on the Cayuse War in an earlier chapter, triggered by the killing of missionary Marcus Whitman and others at the Waiilatpu Mission in 1847. The incident arose from a measles outbreak that devastated the Cayuse, who suspected Whitman's medicine was harming them. U.S. forces demanded the surrender of those responsible, and a series of skirmishes followed. The war did not officially end until around 1855, with the Cayuse forced onto reservations.

Though this conflict began before the large-scale treaty councils, it highlighted the deep mistrust between settlers and tribes. It also showed how disease and cultural misunderstandings could lead to violence. When the later treaties were written, memories of the Cayuse War still lingered on both sides, influencing negotiations.

The Yakama War (1855–1858)

Shortly after signing the treaties at Walla Walla, tensions boiled over into the Yakama War. Settlers and miners, seeking gold, flooded into Yakama lands. Yakama leaders insisted that outsiders respect reservation lines, but few listened. When a Yakama chief was killed by a miner, tribal warriors fought back, attacking those who trespassed.

Governor Stevens called up volunteer militias, while the U.S. Army sent troops to suppress "hostilities." Battles broke out at places like Toppenish Creek. The Yakama, aided by some allied bands, used their knowledge of the terrain to strike military patrols. The war continued for several years, causing destruction on both sides. Ultimately, the government's superior numbers and resources forced the Yakama to retreat or surrender. Many ended up confined to their reservation under strict terms, and their best farmland was opened to settlers.

The Puget Sound War (1855–1856)

Around the same time, conflicts erupted in western Washington, often called the Puget Sound War. Chief Leschi of the Nisqually, angered by the Medicine Creek Treaty's unfair terms, led groups of warriors in attacks on settler homes or military posts. The U.S. Army responded with force, building forts and launching campaigns to capture tribal leaders who resisted.

One notable incident was the Battle of Seattle in January 1856, when a group of Native warriors approached the young town. A U.S. Navy sloop, the USS Decatur, defended the settlement by firing its cannons. Though casualties were low, the event frightened settlers and hardened negative attitudes toward local tribes. Eventually, Chief Leschi was captured and controversially executed. Many later believed Leschi was tried unfairly; his name remains a symbol of Native resistance.

Broken Promises and Hardships

Reservation Realities

For most tribes, life on reservations was harsh. The land was often less fertile than their original territories, making farming difficult. Government annuities arrived late or not at all. Disease outbreaks continued, as many people lived in cramped conditions without adequate medical care. Children were sometimes forced to attend mission or boarding schools where they could not speak their language or follow tribal customs.

In these schools, the U.S. government and church groups aimed to "civilize" Native children, teaching them English and Christianity. Students who resisted could be punished severely. Many children died from illness or malnutrition in overcrowded dormitories. This boarding school system, while more widespread in later decades, had its early roots in this treaty era.

Newcomers Take Over Lands

Meanwhile, settlers, miners, and railroad companies took full advantage of the "open" lands created by treaties. Timber companies harvested forests, farmers fenced off fields, and developers laid down town plots. The idea of Manifest Destiny fueled many Americans' sense that they had a right to expand and profit from these resources. In official government eyes, the treaty obligations were largely met by providing small reservations, small annual payments, and some farm equipment—usually of poor quality.

Native leaders kept sending petitions to territorial or federal authorities, protesting broken treaty clauses. They argued that fishing rights were not being respected, land boundaries were unclear, and that promised supplies never arrived. Few officials listened. With each passing year, the gap widened between what treaties said on paper and what happened in reality.

Resistance After the Wars

Ongoing Struggles for Rights

Even after major wars like the Yakama War or the Puget Sound War ended, many tribes kept fighting for their rights through less violent means. Some leaders traveled to Washington, D.C., to meet with government representatives. They spoke about poor reservation conditions, urging the government to honor old promises. Others tried to use the court system, though early legal cases often ended in favor of the government or big business.

Some tribes adapted by creating new economies within the reservation system—raising livestock, trading crafts, or performing in Wild West shows. Yet, these were not the lifestyles they had known for centuries. The emotional and cultural toll was immense. Ceremonies and languages were sometimes suppressed, though many families kept their traditions alive in private.

Individual Acts of Defiance

Individual acts of defiance also occurred. Some families continued to fish, hunt, or gather foods outside their reservation when they needed to, risking punishment or seizure of their catch. Others refused to send their children to government schools, hiding them from agents. Occasionally, small uprisings flared when local officials pushed too hard or settlers threatened to destroy important burial grounds.

Tribes also formed alliances among themselves, sharing information about good farmland, treaties, or friendly officials. Local gatherings and councils allowed for the exchange of ideas. In some cases, entire communities left reservations to live in more remote areas where they could practice their traditions without immediate interference. This was a difficult path, but it gave them a degree of autonomy.

Profiles of Key Tribal Leaders

Chief Kamiakin (Yakama)

A major figure in the Yakama War, Chief Kamiakin tried to protect his people from the onslaught of settlers and miners. He believed that the Walla Walla treaties unfairly took away most of the Yakama land. While he initially sought peace, he was ready to fight to defend tribal rights. After the Yakama War, Kamiakin fled north, sometimes finding refuge with other tribes in neighboring regions. His resistance and leadership remain a central symbol of Yakama identity.

Chief Leschi (Nisqually)

Leschi opposed the Medicine Creek Treaty because it placed the Nisqually on land far from their river. Feeling betrayed, he led warriors against settlers and U.S. forces in the Puget Sound War. Eventually captured and charged with murder, Leschi was executed in 1858. Many years later, people questioned the fairness of his trial. Modern opinions hold that Leschi was acting as a military leader in a time of war and should not have been tried in a settler court. Eventually, in 2004, his conviction was vacated, symbolically clearing his name long after his death.

Peo Peo Mox Mox (Walla Walla)

Also known as Yellow Bird, Peo Peo Mox Mox was a respected chief of the Walla Walla. He signed treaties at the 1855 council, hoping to secure peace. However, as conflicts grew, tensions between his people and settlers increased. While trying to negotiate or protect his territory, he was taken hostage by volunteer troops, and later killed under disputed circumstances. His death was a tragic reminder of how quickly negotiations could fail when fear and anger dominated.

The Legacy of Treaties and Battles

Ongoing Legal and Cultural Effects

The treaties of the mid-1800s—Medicine Creek, Point Elliott, Walla Walla, and others—became cornerstones of legal disputes that would last well into the future. Clauses guaranteeing fishing and hunting rights eventually led to landmark court cases in the 20th century, where some judges ruled that tribes still retained these rights even after generations of new laws. While these later developments are beyond our immediate historical scope, it is important to note that the words of these treaties had lasting power, despite the immediate period of broken promises.

Culturally, the wars and forced relocations inflicted deep wounds on Native communities. Many lost sacred sites, family burial grounds, and homes they had occupied for centuries. The boarding school era, which ramped up in later decades, further fractured language transmission and family structures. Yet, tribes survived, preserving memories, ceremonies, and ancestral knowledge that continues to define their identity.

Shifting Settler Perspectives

On the settler side, the wars and treaties shaped how people viewed Native tribes for decades to come. Early newspapers often depicted tribes as threats to progress, fueling fear that justified harsh military action. Over time, some settlers recognized the injustices committed, but the majority simply accepted that the land now "belonged" to them. When Washington became a state in 1889, there was little mention in the new constitution about tribal sovereignty, leaving these issues to federal oversight.

Meanwhile, frontier communities grew on lands that once teemed with wildlife and hosted elaborate tribal networks of trade and communication. Newcomers built farms, towns, and roads, rarely acknowledging that these developments sprang directly from treaties that had not been faithfully honored.

U.S. Army and Volunteer Militias

Roles in Suppressing Tribes

During these conflicts, the U.S. Army, along with volunteer militias raised by territorial governors, played a pivotal role in military campaigns. Regular Army officers sometimes tried to follow the rules of engagement set by their superiors, while local militias might act more erratically or brutally, driven by fear or anger. Soldiers built forts—like Fort Walla Walla or Fort Steilacoom—to keep watch over surrounding lands. They patrolled roads and rivers, aiming to protect settlers from tribal raids.

In some instances, Army officers attempted to negotiate peace, but miscommunication or mistrust derailed these efforts. Volunteer militias, lacking formal training, could clash with Army officers about strategy, discipline, or treatment of prisoners. Some volunteers displayed cruelty toward tribal villages, burning homes and destroying winter food supplies to force surrenders.

Forts as Centers of Control

With forts established at key locations, the Army gained a permanent presence in Washington. These forts served as supply stations and bases for expeditionary forces. They also became places where tribes were forced to negotiate or report. As time went on, the forts symbolized the new power structure in the territory: the federal government now had a network of strongholds, further limiting tribal movements.

Economic activity often flourished around these forts. Local merchants sold goods to soldiers, travelers sought lodging, and wagon routes improved. Settlers found comfort in the Army's presence, feeling more secure to plant crops or start businesses. The overall effect was to cement the settler hold on the region, making it less likely that tribal resistance could reverse the massive land grabs.

Peace Efforts and Understanding

Missionaries and Advocates

Despite widespread conflict, certain individuals—missionaries, teachers, traders—worked to ease tensions. Some missionaries genuinely tried to protect Native rights, learning local languages and urging the government to honor treaties. A handful of traders formed friendships with tribal members, bridging cultural gaps. These efforts were small compared to the overall momentum of expansion, but they offered glimpses of the mutual respect that might have been possible under different conditions.

Interpreters and Cultural Mediators

Interpreters played a key role in treaty councils and negotiations, though their skills varied. A good interpreter with knowledge of both languages and cultures could foster real communication, helping each side see the other's point of view. Others, however, were biased or poorly trained, leading to misunderstandings that fueled anger. In a few instances, tribal members who learned English or French at mission schools became their own interpreters, speaking directly on behalf of their people.

Over time, small but steady improvements in cultural understanding took place. Settlers began to realize that tribes had complex social structures and traditions. Tribal leaders recognized that not all settlers were bent on destruction—some truly wanted peaceful trade. Sadly, these mutual realizations often came too late to prevent the violence or stop the land from being taken.

Aftermath and Reflection

Ending Major Wars, Not Tensions

By the late 1850s and early 1860s, the largest conflicts like the Yakama War and the Puget Sound War had cooled. Tribes, weakened by disease, displacement, and military defeat, struggled to hold onto what little land they still controlled. The federal government turned more attention to the Civil War in the East, meaning fewer troops and less money were available for fighting in Washington. This lull did not mean tribal grievances were resolved. Instead, it simply meant that reservations now existed, and any further pushback was met with quick reprisals.

The Seeds of Future Legal Battles

The treaties from this era, though poorly enforced, remained on the books. Generations later, tribal lawyers would point to the fishing and hunting clauses as proof of their continuing rights. Through court cases in the 20th century, some tribes won new recognition of these rights, forcing the state government to respect treaty commitments. These legal victories showed that even though the treaties were overshadowed by conflict at the time, they still held long-term power for Native communities.

Meanwhile, non-Native Washingtonians mostly moved on with building towns, roads, farms, and industries. Many children grew up reading history books that glossed over the details of broken treaties or the forced removal of tribes. Only more recent historical work began to highlight the resilience and determination of Native peoples who navigated these difficult decades.

CHAPTER 14

Boom and Bust – Economic Highs and Lows

By the late 19th century and into the early 20th century, Washington's economy soared at times and struggled at others. Rapid growth in industries like logging, fishing, farming, and mining brought waves of prosperity. Towns became small cities, and people hoped for a bright future filled with jobs and resources. However, these booms often ended in sudden busts, causing unemployment, bankruptcies, and social tension. In this chapter, we will explore the cycles of boom and bust that shaped early Washington. We will see how real estate speculation, resource exploitation, and national financial crises affected local communities. We will also learn about the resilience of people who persevered, rebuilding after each downturn and forging a path toward lasting stability.

Early Booms: Land, Timber, and Railroads

Real Estate Frenzy in the Late 1880s

Just before Washington achieved statehood in 1889, excitement about the territory's potential led to a real estate rush. As railroads expanded, investors predicted that towns like Seattle, Tacoma, and Spokane would explode in population and wealth. Land developers bought large parcels, subdivided them into lots, and sold them at high prices, sometimes without basic infrastructure like roads or water. Advertisements in eastern U.S. newspapers boasted of mild weather, rich soil, and endless opportunities in Washington. Families or single men, lured by these promises, arrived in droves.

In cities, property values soared. Downtown Seattle, for instance, saw buildings rise quickly after the Great Seattle Fire of 1889. Tacoma, the chosen terminus of the Northern Pacific Railroad, expected to rival San Francisco. Spokane became a hub for the inland empire, with wheat fields and mines fueling growth. For a few golden years, people believed they could buy land one week and sell it at a huge profit the next.

Timber Bonanza

Meanwhile, logging continued to boom in western Washington. With massive stands of Douglas fir and cedar, mill owners shipped lumber to California, the Midwest, and even overseas. Sawmills ran day and night, fueling a construction surge in new towns. Steam-powered logging equipment and small rail lines made it easier to harvest remote forests. Seattle became known as a major port for shipping timber, and tiny coastal villages expanded into busy mill towns.

Lumber companies employed thousands, but working conditions were harsh. Accidents were common, wages low, and housing often a bunkhouse near the logging sites. Yet for many, it was a chance to earn money in a growing industry. As forests were cleared, some operators simply moved on to fresh stands elsewhere, leaving behind logged-out land that was difficult to farm. This pattern helped fuel the early economy but set the stage for environmental challenges later on.

Busts and Financial Panics

The Panic of 1893

The first major shock after statehood came with the Panic of 1893, a nationwide economic crisis. Railroad overbuilding, shaky banking practices, and a drop in European investments caused U.S. markets to collapse. Banks failed, factories closed, and thousands lost their jobs. In Washington, the real estate bubble popped. Many who had bought land at inflated prices were suddenly unable to sell or repay loans. Property values plummeted, leaving empty lots and unfinished buildings.

Railroad companies, which had counted on steady traffic and land sales, faced bankruptcy. Construction halted on some lines, and laid-off workers drifted from town to town seeking any work they could find. Sawmills slowed production as demand for lumber fell. Small businesses closed their doors, unable to pay rent or suppliers. The once-confident mood of the late 1880s gave way to worry and frustration.

Mining Slowdowns

Eastern Washington and parts of the Cascade Mountains had also experienced mining booms, especially when gold or silver was discovered. The Panic of 1893 led to falling metal prices, making many mines unprofitable. Investors pulled out, and mining camps became ghost towns. Though some larger mines with stable veins kept operating, most small outfits folded. Communities that relied on these mines saw their local stores and saloons close, and families moved away in search of better prospects elsewhere.

Recovery and Growth Spurts

Wheat and Agriculture Shine

Despite these setbacks, agriculture in Washington steadily expanded, offering a measure of stability. The rolling hills of the Palouse region, around Pullman and Colfax, produced huge wheat crops. Farmers in the Yakima and Wenatchee Valleys developed irrigation projects, turning arid land into orchards for apples, pears, and cherries. As national rail lines became more reliable in the late 1890s, farmers could ship produce to large eastern markets. Though prices for wheat or fruit could fluctuate, many farmers did well enough to improve their equipment and houses.

In areas with good soil and water access, farmers diversified. They raised dairy cows, kept bees, or planted alfalfa hay for livestock feed. This mix of crops helped cushion them from single-crop failures. Granges (farmers' associations) organized communities, shared knowledge, and lobbied the state government for fair railroad rates and better roads. Over time, these agricultural improvements formed a backbone of local economies even when other industries faltered.

Logging Resumes

As the nation recovered from the Panic of 1893, demand for lumber slowly picked up again. Seattle, Tacoma, and other port cities resumed shipping logs and milled wood to distant markets. Timber barons, some from the Midwest, invested in huge tracts of forest. They introduced new machinery, such as donkey engines powered by steam, to haul logs more efficiently. Rail spurs snaked into remote valleys, bringing fresh logs to mills near the water.

With renewed confidence, mill towns expanded, building hotels, saloons, and stores for loggers flush with wages. This second phase of logging growth set the stage for Washington's continuing identity as a timber powerhouse. Yet, it also meant many forests were quickly depleted, leaving questions about sustainability. Few laws limited cutting, and replanting efforts were minimal at best.

The Role of Railroads in Boom and Bust

High Expectations

Railroads were often at the heart of Washington's boom-and-bust cycles. In the 1880s and early 1890s, towns battled to secure a rail connection, offering land or tax breaks to companies in hopes of being on a main line. Land developers advertised any rail-connected town as the "next big thing." People rushed in to open shops, hotels, and boarding houses, expecting a steady flow of travelers and freight.

During booms, rail companies made handsome profits transporting lumber, wheat, fish, and passengers. Stockholders gained, and banks lent money for railroad expansion. However, when national recessions hit or local industries cooled, rail traffic dropped. Maintenance costs ate up profits, leading to bankruptcies. Lines were abandoned, leaving some towns isolated again. These swings proved how vital yet volatile the railroad industry was for early Washington's prosperity.

Competition Among Lines

With multiple major players—the Northern Pacific, Great Northern, and Union Pacific—fighting for routes, competition sometimes caused overbuilding. Companies laid parallel tracks or built expensive tunnels to claim the shortest path across the Cascades. Investors hoped increased traffic would cover these costs, but that traffic did not always materialize. When the economy stumbled, railroads found themselves in deep debt.

Still, railroads remained essential. They allowed farmers to ship their goods to national markets, loggers to move timber efficiently, and workers to reach new job sites. After each bust, lines were reorganized under new management or refinanced by distant bankers. Towns that survived learned to diversify their economies, so they were not entirely dependent on a single railroad or industry.

Fishing and Canning Ups and Downs

Salmon Runs and Cannery Growth

From Puget Sound to the Columbia River, salmon canneries sprang up to process the seemingly endless runs of fish. Investors built canneries near major rivers, employing local workers—both Native and non-Native—to catch, clean, and pack salmon. For a while, it felt like the fish supply would never run out, and the canning business thrived. Exports of canned salmon reached the East Coast and even Europe, creating wealth for cannery owners.

Local economies around cannery sites saw money flow in during the fishing seasons, with fishers spending wages at stores and saloons. Some canneries ran year-round, shifting to other species like shellfish or cod, but salmon was the main draw. This industry fueled smaller booms in coastal areas, supporting boat builders, net makers, and shipping services.

Decline and Regulations

Overfishing soon took its toll. By the late 1890s and early 1900s, salmon numbers in some rivers had dropped sharply. Fish wheels and traps blocked entire channels, capturing huge quantities of salmon before they could spawn. Logging operations further up the rivers caused erosion and habitat destruction, making it harder for salmon to reproduce.

Concerned about losing a vital resource, some voices called for government regulations: limiting the number of traps, restricting fishing seasons, or establishing hatcheries. However, enforcement was weak. Some canneries simply moved to other rivers, repeating the pattern of overfishing. Communities that relied on abundant salmon faced bust cycles when fish stocks collapsed, and cannery owners laid off workers. The problem of balancing profit with conservation would remain a challenge for decades.

Banking, Credit, and Speculation

Frontier Banking Practices

Frontier banks in early Washington operated with fewer regulations than modern financial institutions. They were often founded by local businessmen who used their own capital plus deposits from neighbors. During boom times, these banks readily gave out loans to speculators buying land or to mill owners expanding sawmills. When the economy was hot, everyone seemed to prosper.

But in a bust, depositors rushed to withdraw funds, causing bank runs and collapses. Lacking the backing of a federal reserve system (which did not yet exist in the early territory days), these small banks went under if too many loans defaulted. Entire communities could lose their savings, fueling anger and distrust. Over time, some stable regional banks emerged, but they too were not immune to wider national panics.

Speculative Bubbles

Speculative bubbles formed around various commodities. Real estate was the most common, but others emerged when prices for wheat, silver, or lumber soared beyond reason. Investors far from Washington placed bets on local ventures without fully understanding the risks. Rapid expansion and easy credit fed these bubbles. Once demand cooled or external factors changed—like a national recession—prices crashed, leaving behind empty lots, shuttered businesses, and bankrupt investors.

The cycle repeated: a new discovery or invention (like new logging technology or a promising orchard region) sparked excitement, drawing money and workers. Then a downturn arrived, bringing layoffs and a flood of foreclosures. Some resilient settlers, seeing this pattern, tried to live modestly and avoid heavy debt. Their careful approach spared them the worst of the busts but also limited rapid gains during booms.

Social Impacts of Boom and Bust Cycles

Unemployment and Migration

When mills, mines, or canneries shut down, large groups of workers were left jobless. Many left in search of opportunities elsewhere, traveling by train or steamboat to new logging camps, mines, or growing cities. Towns that once bustled with activity became quiet. Schools lost students, churches lost congregations, and local shops struggled to stay open.

Families that had arrived during a boom found it heartbreaking to abandon their homesteads or small businesses when money dried up. Some tried to switch careers—farmers might become loggers, or mill workers might open a small store. Adapting was not always easy. The harsh reality of the frontier economy tested the grit and determination of those who stayed.

Labor Movements and Strikes

In the late 1800s and early 1900s, workers in logging, mining, and canning started to form labor unions. They demanded better wages, shorter hours, and safer conditions. When booms ended, employers often slashed pay or let workers go without notice. Strikes erupted in certain towns, leading to clashes with owners or local authorities. Even though early union efforts were small and faced opposition, they laid groundwork for future labor movements to challenge the cycle of exploitation during boom times and abandonment during busts.

Attempts at Stabilization and Reform

Early Regulations on Natural Resources

Seeing the destructive nature of unchecked logging or fishing, some territorial and state lawmakers sought to enact controls. A few limited cutting near riverbanks to reduce erosion. Certain open seasons were set for salmon fishing, restricting the time and place for nets or fish wheels. However, powerful business owners resisted strict rules, fearing reduced profits. Enforcement was weak due to lack of funds or political will, so real reform progressed slowly.

Promoting Diversified Economies

Community leaders learned that relying on a single resource or industry made towns vulnerable. They encouraged mixed farming (grain plus livestock plus orchards), small manufacturing, and local markets. Some towns offered incentives for new businesses, like small factories that processed farm goods into cheese or canned fruit. By spreading the economic base, they hoped to blunt the impact of any single industry's downturn.

Railroad companies also encouraged diversification. They promoted land for farming or orchard planting near their lines, reasoning that more settlers would mean more freight and passenger traffic. Newspaper ads in the Midwest or on the East Coast presented Washington as a land of varied resources, from farmland to fisheries to mild climates suitable for fruit trees. Over time, this approach did help towns withstand some of the dramatic shifts in resource-based industries.

Case Studies of Boom and Bust Towns

Seattle's Transformation

Seattle experienced a rapid boom tied to timber and the arrival of the transcontinental rail line in the 1880s. However, the Great Seattle Fire of 1889 destroyed much of downtown. Rather than crumble, the city rebuilt with brick and stone, fueling another boom. When the Panic of 1893 hit, many of Seattle's building projects slowed, but the city soon rebounded by connecting itself to Alaskan gold rushes in the late 1890s. This repeated pattern—disaster followed by opportunity—made Seattle a prime example of resilience during wild economic cycles.

Spokane's Mines and Agriculture

Spokane benefited from proximity to silver and gold mines in Idaho and from wheat fields in the surrounding Palouse region. In the boom years, investors poured money into downtown buildings, street railways, and fancy hotels. When silver prices collapsed in the 1890s, mine closures hurt the city, yet agriculture helped keep it afloat. Over time, Spokane diversified with railroad shops, manufacturing, and trade. While it still felt the bust cycles, the city maintained a steadier path than many purely mining-based settlements.

Logging Towns That Vanished

Numerous logging towns sprung up along rivers in western Washington—places like Bordeaux, Nagrom, and others that might be unfamiliar today. They thrived while the timber lasted, but once the forests were cut, mills closed. Many loggers moved on, leaving behind empty buildings. Some companies simply dismantled housing and took the lumber to the next site. Years later, little remained except rotting foundations and rusted equipment. These ghost towns remind us how a single boom industry could vanish once resources were exhausted.

The Human Spirit and Adaptation

Family and Community Support

Despite repeated setbacks, many Washington residents displayed remarkable perseverance. Neighbors helped each other with food, shelter, or odd jobs. Churches and volunteer groups collected donations for families struck by layoffs. Schools remained open whenever possible, offering a sense of normalcy for children. Women played a big role in sustaining households, managing budgets, sewing clothes, and sometimes earning extra money by taking in boarders or selling baked goods.

Business Innovation

Some entrepreneurs turned adversity into new ideas. If a sawmill closed, a clever mechanic might repurpose the machinery for a grain mill. Fishermen who found salmon runs declining switched to crabbing or shrimping in coastal waters. Owners of idle mines sometimes opened tourist tours of old shafts, appealing to curious travelers. Though these shifts did not always solve broader economic woes, they showed a willingness to adapt rather than give up.

Seeds of Later Changes

Infrastructure Improvements

Boom times often led to improved roads, bridges, and public buildings. Even if a bust followed, the infrastructure remained, helping future growth. For instance, a logging company might build a rail spur that later became a commuter line for a nearby town. A cannery might construct a dock that evolved into a public pier. Over time, these physical assets strengthened local economies, making them more attractive for the next wave of investors.

Shifts in Public Attitude

As Washington moved into the early 1900s, more people recognized the need for stable governance and wise management of resources. Newspapers ran editorials about the dangers of speculation, the importance of reforestation, and the benefit of cooperative grain marketing. While not everyone agreed, the repeated cycles of boom and bust taught painful lessons. Slowly, the public began to accept that short-term profit at the expense of sustainable development could lead to long-term hardship.

Conclusion and Transition

In this chapter, we explored the rollercoaster of economic booms and busts that marked early Washington's path after statehood. Bursts of excitement—fueled by land speculation, logging, fishing, or mining—often ended with painful downturns that left towns scrambling to recover. Yet agriculture, especially in irrigated and grain-producing areas, provided a measure of stability. Railroads connected markets but also carried the risks of overbuilding and financial collapse. Families who endured these cycles showed resilience, supporting each other through tough times and adapting to new opportunities whenever they could.

Understanding this history of economic highs and lows helps us see why Washington eventually turned toward more balanced growth, more careful resource management, and a broader range of industries. In the coming chapters, we will look at early mining adventures in more detail, then explore cultural growth, labor movements, and other social shifts leading into the early 1900s. These developments will reveal how Washington's people continued to carve out a future amidst constant change, drawing on the lessons learned from boom-and-bust eras.

CHAPTER 15

Early Mining Adventures – Searching for Gold and Other Treasures

---

By the mid-1800s, stories of gold strikes and hidden riches tempted many people to try their luck in the hills, streams, and mountains of Washington Territory. Although larger gold rushes occurred in nearby places like California and British Columbia, Washington itself had its share of hopeful miners. They combed riverbeds, built small camps, and carried dreams of finding the next big strike. Other minerals, such as silver, coal, and copper, also drew attention. These mining pursuits boosted the territory's economy, brought in new settlers, and led to the creation of lively, though short-lived, mining towns.

In this chapter, we will explore how early mining adventures shaped Washington. We will see what methods miners used, how mining towns sprang up and sometimes vanished, and why the search for treasure often led to booms and busts. We will also look at the challenges and dangers miners faced as they tunneled underground or panned along rushing rivers. While few struck it rich, their efforts left a mark on local communities and set the stage for future economic developments.

The Lure of Gold

Reports from California and Beyond

The famous California Gold Rush of 1849 sparked the imaginations of people around the world. Thousands headed to California, hoping to find golden nuggets lying in riverbeds. As news spread that precious metals might also exist in Oregon Country and further north, some adventurers veered off to explore Washington's river valleys and mountainous regions. Even small rumors of gold could trigger a rush of optimistic fortune seekers.

Miners carried pickaxes, pans, and simple sluice boxes. They set out on foot or by horseback, following faint trails or forging new paths into remote canyons. Some had experience from California or other goldfields; others were complete newcomers, guided only by stories overheard in saloons or read in newspaper notices. While California overshadowed Washington in sheer numbers of prospectors, the territory still saw plenty of determined adventurers eager for a lucky break.

Early Indications of Gold

In the 1850s, fur trappers, missionaries, and traders occasionally mentioned seeing signs of gold in streams. Small-scale panning along rivers like the Columbia or the Snake produced modest yields. By the late 1850s and early 1860s, a few minor strikes caught public attention. Though not as dramatic as the gold finds in California or the Fraser Canyon in British Columbia, these small discoveries hinted that Washington's geology might hold hidden treasure.

Local newspapers fanned the excitement, printing stories of men who found a few ounces of gold dust in a creek bed. Since the territory was still young, officials did not have many regulations in place to manage mining claims. Prospectors tended to follow informal rules, staking out a stretch of land along a river or gulch and hoping no one else jumped their claim.

The Methods of Early Mining

Panning and Sluicing

In the early stages, most prospectors used simple techniques like panning. They scooped gravel and dirt from riverbeds into a pan, then swirled it in water, letting the lighter material wash away. If tiny flakes of gold were present, they settled at the bottom. This process was slow, backbreaking work, performed kneeling on riverbanks for hours. While a skilled miner could spot fine flecks of gold, it often took many pans just to gather a small amount of dust.

When a river showed decent gold content, groups of miners built sluice boxes. These were wooden troughs that channeled water and gravel over riffles (small slats of wood) in the bottom. Gold particles, heavier than sand or gravel, settled behind these riffles, making it easier to collect the precious metal. Sluicing sped up production, but it required a steady flow of water and enough hands to shovel. Miners who pooled their efforts could process more material each day.

Underground and Hard Rock Mining

Where gold or other minerals were locked in veins of solid rock, miners had to blast or chisel their way into hillsides or tunnels. This style of "hard rock" mining required heavier tools like drills, picks, and black powder for explosions. After breaking up the rock, miners hauled it out in carts or sacks to stamp mills, which crushed the ore, releasing gold or silver inside.

These operations were riskier than panning. Tunnels could collapse if not properly shored with timber supports. Coal miners and hard rock miners also faced the danger of toxic gases, flooding, and sudden cave-ins. Candlelight or simple oil lamps lit their way underground, limiting visibility. Despite the hazards, some ventured deeper to reach rich veins. Over time, a few larger mining companies formed to handle big projects, raising money from investors who hoped for significant returns.

Key Mining Regions in Washington

Northeastern Washington

The northeastern corner of Washington, near present-day Stevens and Ferry Counties, became a small hotbed of mining activity. Prospectors found gold along the upper Columbia River and its tributaries. Towns like Colville served as supply centers for scattered mining camps deeper in the mountains. Some miners also sought silver, lead, and other minerals in rugged terrain where heavy snowfall limited operations much of the year.

Small diggings sometimes grew into semi-permanent camps with crude cabins, a saloon or two, and a general store. During winter, miners often left the high country, returning in spring when snows melted and water levels in streams ran high enough for panning or sluicing. This seasonal rhythm shaped life in many mining communities.

Cascade Mountain Foothills

The Cascade Range provided its own opportunities, especially along rivers that carried eroded particles from mineral-rich rock. Places like the Skykomish, Snoqualmie, and Nooksack Rivers saw prospectors setting up simple camps. While large strikes were rare, a few persistent individuals claimed moderate success. Hiking through dense forests and steep canyons was tough. Some miners used mule trains to carry in supplies and haul out sacks of ore.

Conditions in these mountains could be harsh—heavy rains, fast-rising rivers, and winter snows that cut off camps for months. Yet the scenery was beautiful, and rumors of a hidden "mother lode" kept people searching. As logging also pushed into these regions, some loggers took part-time roles as prospectors, blending the two livelihoods in the hope of extra income.

Columbia River and Tributaries

Along the main stem of the Columbia, as well as the Okanogan and Methow Rivers, miners sifted river gravels for fine gold. These areas sometimes rewarded patient efforts with small but steady pay. Towns like Okanogan and Oroville became stopping points for prospectors traveling between Washington and British Columbia, where large gold rushes (like the Fraser Canyon rush) had drawn international attention. Some miners crossing the border paused in Washington, tried their luck, and either stayed or continued north if prospects fizzled out.

The Rise of Coal, Silver, and Other Minerals

Coal Mining in Western Washington

While gold captured imaginations, coal often provided more consistent income for some communities. By the 1870s and 1880s, coal deposits near places like Black Diamond, Roslyn, and Wilkeson fueled the region's growing need for energy. Railroads used coal to power steam locomotives, and towns burned it for heat. Coal mining required a different approach than gold panning—workers dug deep tunnels, used safety lamps to watch for flammable gases, and built strong timber supports to prevent cave-ins.

Companies formed to operate large coal mines, hiring hundreds of workers. These miners faced tough conditions underground, chipping away at coal seams and loading railcars. When production was high, entire towns flourished with boarding houses, schools, and shops. However, collapses or gas explosions could kill many at once, and economic downturns led to layoffs. Still, coal remained a staple resource, supporting the railroads and local industries well into the 20th century.

Silver and Lead in the Metal Mines

In addition to gold, parts of Washington contained silver and lead ores, often found together. The metal mines around Lake Chelan and in northeastern regions drew investors who built stamp mills to crush ore. Shipments of silver-rich rock traveled by wagon or rail to smelters, sometimes located outside the territory. Mining stocks soared if a discovery seemed promising, but when assays showed less metal than hoped, prices sank fast.

Small boomtowns sprang up near these silver strikes. Buildings went up quickly, often of flimsy construction. Merchants sold supplies at high prices, expecting to make quick profits before miners moved on. If the veins ran dry or proved too costly to extract, the town might dwindle to only a few residents. This pattern of sudden growth followed by abrupt decline repeated itself in many silver-mining districts.

Boomtowns and Their Way of Life

Rowdy Camps and Sudden Growth

When a rumor of a promising strike spread, prospectors rushed in. They threw together tents, lean-tos, or crude log huts. The sound of hammers and saws often filled the air as new arrivals built saloons and boarding houses. A typical mining boomtown might have one or two dusty streets lined with wooden structures. Signs reading "Assayer," "Dry Goods," and "Miner's Supply" beckoned customers. Saloons served as central meeting places, offering whiskey, card games, and sometimes rowdy entertainment.

Law enforcement in these towns was minimal. A local sheriff or a self-appointed marshal might try to keep order, but drunken brawls, claim-jumping disputes, and petty theft were common. Justice often followed the rules of mining districts, where informal committees settled who owned which claim or how water rights would be divided. Many residents planned to stay only as long as the gold or silver held out. Once pay dirt was scarce, they packed up and moved on to the next rumored bonanza.

Hardships and Daily Struggles

Though some newspapers romanticized mining life, reality was harsh. Fresh food was scarce and expensive, especially in remote camps. Cans of beans, salt pork, and coffee became diet staples. Sewage systems and clean water were rare, spreading diseases like dysentery or cholera. Winters might trap people in their cabins with dwindling supplies of firewood and food. Summers brought dust, heat, and swarms of biting insects.

Mining tools wore out quickly. Picks needed frequent sharpening, pans got dented, and boots tore on rocky terrain. Injuries were common—sprained ankles on rough trails, crushed fingers under falling rock, or burns from black powder mishaps. Medical help might be days away, so friends or neighbors had to act as nurses. In some camps, there were no women at all, leaving men to cook and mend clothes. In others, a few families braved the conditions, raising children among the clamor of picks and blasting powder.

Native Peoples and Mining Encroachment

Overlapping Land Claims

Much like settlers and farmers, miners often disregarded tribal territories when they rushed in for gold or silver. They set up camps on lands that treaties had promised to Native Tribes or next to fishing and hunting grounds crucial to tribal survival. Some tribes tried to charge miners a fee for passing through or using certain areas, but most were ignored or met with hostility.

Tensions flared in regions where miners polluted rivers or chopped down forests for timbers without regard to tribal resource needs.

Tribal leaders sometimes demanded the U.S. government remove illegal mining camps. Officials often turned a blind eye, focusing on economic development instead. As a result, treaties that had already been poorly enforced became even more neglected, widening the gap between tribes and the incoming population.

Cooperative or Dependent Relationships

In some cases, tribes and miners found ways to cooperate. Native guides, with deep knowledge of the terrain, led prospectors to safe river crossings or hidden passes. Tribes sometimes traded fresh game or fish for mining tools or other goods. A few tribal members even tried panning or sluicing themselves, seeking gold to trade for clothing or supplies. However, overall, mining expansions contributed to the broader theme of displacement. As more non-Native people arrived, the pressure on tribal lands and resources intensified.

Environmental Impacts and Early Reactions

Damaged Streams and Forests

Mining practices took a toll on the environment. Hydraulic mining, used in some areas (though more common in California), involved blasting hillsides with high-pressure water, washing away soil and gravel into riverbeds. This silt clogged streams, harming fish habitats. Even simpler methods like panning and sluicing disturbed riverbanks. Timber demands for mine supports led to more deforestation, and the use of toxic chemicals, such as mercury or arsenic to extract gold, polluted waterways.

Local people who depended on clean rivers for drinking or fishing noticed changes quickly. Fish populations declined, and muddy water made daily chores harder. Some complained to territorial officials or newspapers, but few regulations existed. With Washington's economy eager to expand, those in power tended to side with miners, trusting the land could handle the stress or believing short-term gains outweighed long-term harm.

Calls for Responsible Mining (Small but Significant)

Even in this era, a few voices urged caution. Certain newspaper editorials warned against reckless hydraulic mining or the dumping of tailings in rivers. Some farmers whose fields were ruined by silt demanded compensation. Nevertheless, formal environmental laws would not appear until much later. Most miners followed the easiest path to profits, moving on when the land was no longer profitable. The land itself bore the scars—stripped hillsides, gouged-out creek beds, and abandoned pits.

Financing Mining Ventures

Individual Prospectors vs. Companies

During the earliest days of each rush, individual prospectors dominated. They arrived with minimal equipment and staked personal claims. If word got out that a claim was producing well, outside investors might buy it from the prospector and bring in bigger equipment or more workers. Over time, some claims were consolidated under small companies, which could afford stamp mills or heavy machinery. This meant more efficient extraction of gold or silver—but also higher stakes.

Companies sold shares to investors, sometimes inflating claims of the mine's riches. When returns failed to meet promises, stock prices crashed. A single bad assay report could sink a venture, leaving mine owners and workers unpaid. Meanwhile, savvy businesspeople who sold their shares at the peak might profit handsomely. These ups and downs echoed the broader pattern of boom-and-bust economics that shaped Washington's growth.

Bank Loans and Eastern Investors

Local banks in growing towns like Spokane, Seattle, or Walla Walla sometimes loaned money to small mining outfits, using equipment or claims as collateral. They hoped a rich strike would lead to big loan repayments with interest. Large-scale projects needed more capital, so promoters traveled to San Francisco, New York, or even Europe, pitching Washington's potential. Brochures showcased scenic mountains and glowing testimonies about the wealth just waiting to be mined.

Still, many investors lost money when ore veins proved shallow or difficult to extract. The unpredictability of geology, combined with shaky business practices, ensured that only a fraction of mines turned consistent profits. Nonetheless, each discovery cycle lured fresh capital, shaping entire local economies around the possibility of hitting the mother lode.

Declines and Shifting Fortunes

Exhausted Sites and Abandoned Towns

Over time, many of the easy-to-reach gold deposits were worked out. Sluices stopped yielding enough dust to pay for food and supplies. Hard rock mines followed veins deeper underground until it became too expensive or unsafe to continue. Coal mines sometimes flooded, caved in, or faced competition from newly discovered fields in other parts of the territory. When a mine closed, the surrounding town often collapsed economically.

People who had arrived in a burst of optimism found themselves jobless or stuck with worthless property. General stores, saloons, and hotels shut their doors. Local newspapers folded, and the population scattered to find new prospects. Some ghost towns left behind a handful of stubborn residents or families with nowhere else to go. Others vanished entirely, reclaimed by the forest or the desert.

Shifting to Other Industries

By the late 1800s, logging, fishing, and agriculture had become more stable industries in many parts of Washington. Skilled miners sometimes transitioned to work in sawmills or on farms. Towns that diversified—supporting both a mining trade and local farming—fared better than those that relied solely on one silver or gold discovery. Railroads helped by transporting orchard produce or timber, cushioning some communities from the worst mining downturns.

Nevertheless, the dream of striking it rich through mining never fully disappeared. Even as large-scale mining waned, small operations or prospectors with pans continued searching remote creeks or old mine tailings for overlooked pockets of gold. The territory's (and later the state's) leaders encouraged ongoing exploration, hoping for new discoveries that might spark another economic upswing.

Stories of Notable Finds and Failures

The Rock Candy Mountain Legend

Local folklore often mentioned a mythical "Rock Candy Mountain," rumored to be covered with quartz crystals or precious gems. Though no one ever found such a place, the legend spurred adventurous souls to wander deep into Washington's wilderness, imagining glittering treasures. Some claimed they found sparkling rocks that turned out to be common quartz. Others insisted the real location remained hidden, leading future generations on fruitless quests.

The Mystery of Miner John

Another tale told of "Miner John," a lone prospector who supposedly found a rich gold vein in the Cascades. He returned to town with a bag full of nuggets and quietly paid for supplies, then vanished back into the hills. When he never reappeared, rumors spread that he had died or been lost in a storm. Treasure hunters occasionally tried to trace his steps, but no conclusive find emerged. The story symbolized the elusive nature of fortune: a brief glimpse of wealth, then nothing.

These anecdotes, shared around campfires and in local papers, fueled the romance of mining. Even with so many hardships and failures, the idea that anyone could discover a hidden fortune kept pulling people toward the mountains and streams of Washington.

Lasting Effects on Washington's Development

Infrastructure and Transportation

Mining ventures spurred early roads and trails, allowing pack trains and wagons to reach remote valleys. Rail lines sometimes extended closer to mining districts, hoping to haul out ore or bring in heavy equipment. Even after mining camps declined, these transportation routes benefited farmers, loggers, and other settlers. Some of today's highways in mountainous areas trace the paths first carved by miners a century or more ago.

Boost to Local Economies

Although many individuals lost money, the overall effect of early mining on Washington's economy was not entirely negative. Mining camps needed supplies—food, tools, lumber, clothing—supporting local merchants. Sawmills, boat operators, and freight haulers found customers in miners. Some small ports developed because steamboats carried gear upriver to distant camps. In turn, certain towns became permanent trading centers even if the original mine that sparked their growth faded out.

Moreover, mining laid a foundation for future industrial growth. Skills learned in tunnel construction helped shape knowledge for building railroad tunnels. The presence of coalfields encouraged the rise of railroads, steamships, and city heating. Though gold or silver might have run out, the territory gained an experience in harnessing its natural resources—sometimes for better, sometimes for worse.

Miners' Lives and Cultural Impact

Diversity in Mining Camps

Mining camps attracted people from many backgrounds. White Americans from the eastern states mingled with immigrants from Ireland, Germany, Italy, and Scandinavia. Chinese workers, sometimes driven away from larger rushes elsewhere, set up laundry businesses or worked claims. African American miners also arrived, though they often faced discrimination. This mix of cultures led to varied foods, music, and traditions in camp gatherings.

Tensions could arise—racial prejudice, language barriers, and competition for claims sometimes resulted in fights or forced expulsions. But in many camps, necessity forged a sense of cooperation. If a tunnel collapsed, everyone pitched in to rescue those trapped. If a group of miners fell sick, neighbors pooled resources to help. Though relations were not always harmonious, the shared hardships bound people together in unique ways.

Entertainment and Social Life

Miners found ways to have fun despite grueling work. Saloons hosted card games, dancing, and occasional live music by fiddlers or pianists. Traveling performers or medicine shows drifted through, offering a break from daily labor. Some camps built makeshift theaters or staged minstrel shows. Newspaper readers followed national news of bigger gold strikes in places like the Klondike (in the 1890s) or read tall tales about "lost mines" in the southwestern deserts.

Religious services also took place if a preacher happened to pass by. In a few areas, mission churches set up small chapels, inviting miners to Sunday gatherings. Holidays like the Fourth of July inspired day-long celebrations with foot races, shooting contests, or feasts of whatever food the camp could gather. Such festivities gave miners a taste of normalcy in an otherwise rugged existence.

Looking to the Future

Transition to Larger-Scale Operations

By the turn of the 20th century, many small-scale mining efforts had either dried up or been replaced by bigger operations financed by companies. These companies employed engineers and geologists, applying more advanced technology like compressed-air drills or early dynamite charges. With greater resources and scientific approaches, they could reach deeper veins or process lower-grade ore profitably. However, they also demanded stable markets, and global fluctuations in metal prices influenced whether these mines stayed open.

In coal mining, major corporations like the Northern Pacific Railroad heavily invested in extracting fuel for trains and city power plants. This shift meant miners were often employees rather than independent prospectors, leading to labor disputes and union organization efforts. Washington's identity as a place of varied resources continued to evolve, shaped by corporate strategies as well as local community goals.

Legacy of the Search for Treasure

Although the number of big gold or silver strikes in Washington was fewer than in some neighboring regions, the persistent efforts of miners left behind a cultural memory of adventure and possibility. Ghost towns, old mine shafts, and rusted equipment dot the landscape, reminding future generations of the intense drive that once led people into the mountains. Local museums sometimes display the battered pans, picks, and maps these miners used, teaching visitors about an era of raw hope and tenacious spirit.

Today's understanding of Washington's history must include the passion—and sometimes folly—of early mining ventures. Even as modern industries replaced the pick-and-pan approach, the quest for hidden riches shaped roads, towns, and population movements. And while many miners walked away with empty pockets, their stories remain woven into the broader tapestry of how Washington came to be.

CHAPTER 16

Cultural Growth – Churches, Newspapers, and Community Activities

---

By the late 1800s and early 1900s, Washington's society was transforming from a loose collection of frontier settlements into more organized communities with shared traditions and institutions. While logging, fishing, farming, and mining shaped local economies, churches, newspapers, and various social gatherings shaped hearts and minds. These cultural elements helped tie people together, giving them ways to communicate, celebrate, and support one another. In this chapter, we will see how churches multiplied and adapted in different regions, how newspapers connected distant towns, and how community activities—from dances to lectures—brought people together.

Churches: Faith and Community

Early Mission Influence

In Washington's earliest days, missionaries built small chapels to spread their religious beliefs among Native peoples and settlers alike. We have seen how these missions sometimes clashed with local tribes. As the territory grew, missionaries also provided services to the growing settler population, holding Sunday gatherings in mission buildings or in someone's home if no church existed. Missionaries often doubled as teachers or medical helpers, bringing reading lessons or basic health care alongside religious teaching.

With time, different denominations took root. Catholics established parishes in urban centers and remote logging areas, while Protestant groups—Methodists, Baptists, Presbyterians, and Congregationalists—raised small chapels in homestead regions. Each congregation reflected the backgrounds and beliefs of the settlers in that area. Lutheran churches sprang up in towns with Scandinavian immigrants, for instance, and Catholic missions continued to serve French Canadian trappers or Irish railroad workers.

Building Churches in Town

As towns grew, residents wanted more permanent places of worship. They donated lumber, glass windows, and their own labor to construct church buildings. A typical frontier church was modest, with wooden walls and a simple steeple. Inside, rows of benches or homemade pews faced a small pulpit, lit by lanterns or early gas lamps. Church bells rang out on Sunday mornings, calling families from outlying farms or from crowded boarding houses.

Services provided moral guidance and a sense of unity. Ministers spoke of faith but also commented on local issues—road building, saloon closures, or help for the poor. Churches hosted weddings, funerals, and holiday celebrations like Christmas or Easter programs. For many families, the church was the social heart of the community, a place where neighbors could gather and catch up on the week's news.

Newspapers: Spreading Information and Ideas

Early Printing Presses

Printing presses in Washington arrived alongside the earliest settlers, though they were initially rare. Small territorial newspapers circulated in places like Olympia, Steilacoom, and Vancouver by the 1850s. These papers might be published weekly or biweekly, depending on the availability of news and supplies.

Editor-publishers were often spirited individuals who printed political opinions, local gossip, and advertisements for everything from horse auctions to new store openings.

Hand-cranked presses required time and effort to set type by hand. Printers used lead pieces bearing letters (type), arranged them into words, and inked them before pressing paper sheets onto the surface. Mistakes were easy to make, and news was sometimes days or weeks old by the time it reached readers. Still, these newspapers provided a vital link in the territory—especially when roads were muddy and telegraphs not yet reliable in all areas.

Growth of Local Journalism

As communities expanded, so did the number of newspapers. Each town wanted its own "voice" to share local events, city council decisions, and social notes like births, weddings, or funerals. Editors sometimes took strong political stances, supporting or opposing regional leaders. Rival newspapers in the same town could engage in feisty debates, hurling editorial insults across the pages. Even small logging or mining camps might support a newspaper for a while if local businesses bought enough ads.

Readers eagerly awaited the arrival of each issue, scanning headlines for news of railroad developments, shipping schedules, or upcoming dances and fairs. Farmers looked for crop prices, while workers checked for job listings. Gossip columns told who had arrived on the latest stagecoach or which family was hosting out-of-town visitors. These local tidbits knitted communities together, making people feel connected even if they lived miles apart.

Community Activities and Gatherings

Dances, Picnics, and Barn Raisings

Away from work in fields, mills, or mines, settlers craved opportunities to socialize and have fun. Community dances were common, taking place in a town hall, church basement, or even a large barn cleared of hay bales. A fiddle player or a small band provided music, and couples whirled around in waltzes or square dances. Everyone—young and old—attended, sometimes bringing potluck dishes to share. These events let neighbors catch up, forge friendships, and even spark romances.

Picnics and harvest festivals celebrated the fruits of labor. Families packed baskets with bread, pies, cold chicken, and fresh produce. They spread blankets in a meadow or near a creek, enjoying group games like tug-of-war or three-legged races. A local choir might sing patriotic songs or hymns. Barn raisings showcased the frontier spirit of cooperation: men gathered to erect a barn's framework in a single day, while women prepared hearty meals. Even children helped carry small tools or fetch water. These gatherings taught everyone the value of working together.

Literary Societies and Lectures

Not all social events involved dancing or feasting. Some communities formed literary societies where members discussed books or held debates. These meetings took place in schools, churches, or even general stores after hours. People read aloud from newspapers or novels, then shared opinions. For many, it was the only chance to hear new ideas or practice public speaking, especially if they had limited schooling.

Traveling lecturers or educators occasionally toured the territory, speaking on topics like science, geology, or social reform. They might set up in a schoolhouse and charge a small fee for admission. Curious settlers attended, eager for intellectual stimulation. Some lectures promoted temperance, warning against the dangers of alcohol. Others showcased wonders like electricity or new inventions, capturing imaginations about future possibilities.

Ethnic and Immigrant Communities

Cultural Traditions

Washington's population included people from many backgrounds: Germans, Swedes, Norwegians, Italians, Irish, and more. Each group brought unique customs, food, and celebrations. Lutheran churches in Scandinavian communities celebrated holidays like St. Lucia Day, featuring candlelit processions. German clubs organized festivals with sausage, beer, and traditional dances. Irish immigrants honored St. Patrick's Day with parades or gatherings.

In larger towns, neighborhoods formed around shared language or heritage. People built ethnic halls where they could host dances, weddings, or social events that reminded them of their homelands. These halls often doubled as informal job centers, where newcomers got tips on local work. Though English was the main public language, mother tongues thrived in homes and community gatherings. This diversity enriched social life, giving everyone a taste of global traditions.

Embracing New Identities

Over time, second-generation children blended old country traditions with American experiences. They joined local churches, read English newspapers, and attended territorial or state schools. Yet they might also learn their parents' language at home. Ethnic organizations helped them stay connected to cultural roots through music, costumes, and dances. Some newspapers were published in foreign languages, such as Swedish or German, catering to older immigrants who never became fluent in English.

While prejudice existed, many towns also realized that diverse cultures could benefit everyone—through shared recipes, crafts, or even new ways to celebrate holidays. Small shops selling specialty goods, like Italian olive oil or Norwegian herring, popped up in growing cities. This mix of traditions shaped Washington's evolving identity, showing that despite different origins, people could find common ground in hard work, faith, and community ties.

Women's Roles and Social Impact

Organizing Clubs and Societies

Women in frontier and early statehood communities were often at the heart of social life. They formed sewing circles, cooking clubs, and charitable groups. These gatherings allowed them to share skills, from quilting to preserving fruits, while also discussing family or town matters. Churches relied heavily on women to run Sunday schools and plan events. Many towns had a Ladies' Aid Society that collected donations for widows, built church pews, or helped families rebuild after fires.

Over time, some women's clubs expanded to include reading rooms or literary discussions, evolving into more formal institutions. They hosted lectures on art or music, encouraging a level of cultural refinement. Through these clubs, women also learned leadership skills and organized campaigns for community improvements—like raising money for a local library or pushing for cleaner streets. Even before they had full voting rights, women influenced local decisions by mobilizing neighbors around good causes.

Advocating for Suffrage

While Washington women did not gain the right to vote in the state constitution of 1889, they did not give up. Suffrage leaders emerged, organizing rallies and writing newspaper columns. They argued that women who worked hard in homes, farms, and schools should have a say in laws that affected their families. Some religious groups supported women's suffrage, seeing it as a moral cause. Others resisted, worried that giving women the vote would disrupt traditional roles.

Gradually, the suffrage movement built momentum. Communities debated the issue, and men began to see women as partners in shaping the new state. Although full suffrage came in 1910 (beyond the immediate scope of this chapter), these early social clubs and church groups laid the groundwork by teaching women organizational skills and providing them a public voice. In the meantime, women continued to make strong contributions to local culture and family life.

The Role of Fraternal Orders and Societies

Lodges and Brotherhoods

Men often joined fraternal orders such as the Masons, Odd Fellows, Knights of Pythias, or the Improved Order of Red Men. These groups offered a sense of camaraderie and ritual. Lodge meetings took place in dedicated halls, where members performed ceremonies, supported each other in times of need, and sometimes engaged in secret handshakes or symbols. While the specifics varied, the idea was to build moral character, mutual assistance, and community respect.

Lodges hosted social events like balls, parades, and banquets, inviting local families to share in the festivities. Initiation rites and hierarchical degrees appealed to many who missed the structured social life of older states or their countries of origin. Being a lodge member could also provide business connections, as members often preferred to trade with or hire fellow lodge brothers.

Mutual Aid and Community Projects

Beyond ceremony, these orders provided real help. If a member fell ill or died, the lodge collected money for medical bills or funeral costs. Widows could receive aid, and children might be offered scholarships if the lodge was prosperous enough. During disasters, lodge members organized relief, delivering food or blankets. This helped fill gaps left by a young state government still lacking extensive social services.

While some critics saw lodges as exclusive or secretive, many towns benefited from the charitable works they did. Lodges sometimes built libraries, sponsored orphans, or led drives to improve roads. By combining social interaction with charitable aims, these fraternal orders grew in popularity, leaving a distinctive mark on Washington's social fabric.

Education and Libraries

Advancements in Schooling

Although one-room schoolhouses dominated early education, larger towns began to establish multi-room schools with separate grades as the population increased. Teachers organized extracurricular clubs—like debate teams or drama societies—to give students broader learning experiences. Some towns formed high schools, which was a significant step, as most teenagers previously went to work by that age.

Churches or civic groups sometimes funded night classes for adults who never had the chance to learn reading and writing. This helped immigrants improve their English. In logging or mining camps, if a permanent school did not exist, traveling teachers might set up temporary classes, staying a few months before moving on. As the state matured, official laws required more consistent school attendance, reflecting the new priority placed on education.

Public Libraries and Traveling Libraries

Libraries were still relatively rare, but a few towns managed to set them up—sometimes as part of a reading room in a church basement or above a mercantile store. Civic-minded citizens donated books or funds to buy them. Readers could borrow novels, histories, or reference works, returning them within a set time. Clubs hosted "library socials" to raise money for new volumes.

Traveling libraries emerged in certain counties. A teacher or volunteer might load a trunk with books and carry it by wagon to remote farms. Families could borrow books for a month and then pass the trunk along. This system offered people in isolated areas a taste of literature and learning. Such efforts bridged the distance between more developed towns and scattered homesteads, uniting them under the love of reading.

Civic Celebrations and Holidays

Fourth of July and Pioneer Days

By the time Washington became a state, the Fourth of July had solidly entrenched itself as the prime public holiday. Towns organized parades with horses, wagons, and homemade floats. Brass bands played patriotic tunes, while children waved small flags. Speeches by local politicians or war veterans filled the air, praising the nation's ideals and the state's bright future. Booths sold ice cream, lemonade, and candies. At night, fireworks lit the sky if funds allowed.

Some communities also celebrated "Pioneer Days," honoring the region's earlier settlers. People dressed in old-time costumes, reenacting how the territory looked in the 1850s or 1860s. Children marveled at old wagons or listened to stories about days without railroads or telegraphs. These events aimed to build pride in local history, reminding newcomers that the towns they saw now sprang from a few hardy pioneers' efforts.

County Fairs and Agricultural Shows

Rural counties developed annual fairs where farmers showcased prized livestock—cattle, pigs, and poultry—and displayed produce like giant pumpkins or perfect ears of corn. Quilts, baked goods, and jams were also judged. Ribbons or small cash prizes went to winners, and bragging rights lasted all year. These fairs drew families from miles around, giving them a break from daily chores and a reason to celebrate.

Carnival attractions—pony rides, game booths, or fortune-tellers—added excitement. The fairs offered a chance to see new farming equipment or seeds, shared by traveling salesmen who set up stalls. Neighbors swapped tips for irrigation, pest control, or orchard care. In this way, agricultural knowledge spread, ensuring that Washington's farming communities kept growing stronger.

Communication Through Letters and Telegraph

Letters and Mail Delivery

While newspapers spread local events, personal letters let people maintain ties with faraway relatives or sweethearts. Post offices were essential in each town, often located inside a general store or a stand-alone building with a wooden sign. Stagecoaches or horseback riders delivered mail along routes that might take days or weeks. A single letter traveling from the East Coast to Washington could pass through multiple territories before arriving.

Mail days were big events. People lined up at the post office, hoping for news from home. Letters might contain births, deaths, recipes, or advice about business opportunities. Those who couldn't write relied on a literate neighbor or official scribe to help them. Receiving or sending mail helped settlers feel less isolated, bridging the distance between them and the places they'd left behind.

Telegraph Connections

By the 1860s and 1870s, telegraph lines reached some parts of Washington, enabling faster communication. Telegraph operators in towns tapped out messages in Morse code, sending them to larger stations that relayed them to distant cities. Urgent business news—like a sale of land or a change in lumber prices—traveled more quickly this way. Though telegrams were expensive, big companies or newspapers used them to stay current. Smaller farmers or homesteaders generally stuck to letters or face-to-face visits.

The telegraph also helped coordinate railroad schedules, ensuring trains met at stations without major delays. Over time, these lines expanded, linking more communities and fostering a sense that Washington was truly connected to the national grid. Still, the telegraph could be unreliable in remote areas, where storms knocked down lines or local offices lacked trained operators.

The Growth of Shared Identity

Forming a Statewide Consciousness

As churches, newspapers, schools, and social clubs flourished, people began to think of themselves not just as residents of a single town but as part of a larger region—Washington. They read about events in other counties, recognized shared problems (like road conditions), and followed state politics in Olympia. Churches held regional conferences, sending ministers to build unity among scattered congregations. Newspapers reprinted articles from one another, broadening readers' perspectives.

Local celebrations like the Fourth of July or pioneer reunions helped cement a collective identity, reminding everyone that, despite different backgrounds, they had shaped the territory—and, after 1889, the state—together. Town councils coordinated with county officials on projects like bridging rivers or improving stage roads, further linking communities into a network of mutual interests. This growing sense of belonging to a unified place contrasted sharply with the earlier frontier days, when settlements were often isolated and focused on survival.

Impact on Politics and Social Causes

These cultural ties also affected how residents approached social issues. Temperance, labor rights, and women's suffrage all benefited from the expanding platforms of churches, newspapers, and civic clubs. A traveling speaker could spark debates in multiple towns within a few months, uniting people who discovered they cared about the same reforms. Petitions circulated more easily, and newspapers printed editorials supporting or opposing certain bills in the state legislature.

As a result, grassroots campaigns influenced lawmakers in Olympia. For example, a wave of church-led petitions might push for Sunday closing laws or restrictions on alcohol sales. Articles in newspapers could expose harsh conditions in logging camps, leading to calls for protective legislation. Over time, these efforts shaped early labor laws, educational funding, and other policies that steered Washington's growth.

Challenges and Divisions

Religious Differences and Conflicts

While churches generally united people, tensions arose when different denominations clashed over doctrine or competition for members. Some towns saw sharp debates over whether to allow saloons, or whether Sunday should be a day of rest with no business. Clergy who preached fiery sermons against "worldly behavior" upset those who enjoyed dancing or card games. Conversely, more liberal ministers faced criticism from conservative congregations. This friction sometimes split communities along religious lines, though most found ways to coexist for the sake of harmony.

Racial and Ethnic Barriers

Despite a growing sense of shared identity, prejudice and discrimination persisted. Chinese workers, for instance, faced legal restrictions and sometimes violence. African Americans had limited employment options beyond menial jobs, and few towns welcomed them openly. Native peoples were largely confined to reservations, their cultural gatherings rarely recognized by the wider community. While certain churches or newspapers called for tolerance, old biases lingered. Many immigrants stuck to enclaves where they felt safe, rarely mixing with other groups. This reality tempered the ideals of unity that civic events often promoted.

A Bridge Between Frontier and Future

The Emergence of Civic Pride

By the early 1900s, many Washington towns had established churches, newspapers, schools, clubs, and libraries as pillars of daily life. Town pride took shape in well-kept main streets, neat school buildings, and congregations that organized charity drives or improvement projects. Local boosters boasted about their communities in pamphlets sent east, praising the moral, intellectual, and social strengths of their "modern" towns. This booster spirit helped attract newcomers, convinced that Washington was not just a wild frontier but a place to build a refined life.

Seeds of Modernization

Infrastructure improvements—such as telegraph lines, better roads, and in some places early electricity—gradually changed how people lived. Churches installed small pipe organs or replaced lanterns with electric bulbs (when that technology reached them). Newspapers expanded in size, printing more pages and adding photographs. Social clubs branched out into new themes, like horticulture or photography, reflecting evolving interests. All these shifts hinted that Washington was transitioning from a rugged territory to a maturing state with broader cultural aspirations.

CHAPTER 17

Early 1900s Changes – Labor Movements and Social Shifts

By the dawn of the 1900s, Washington was no longer a young frontier territory. It was a state with growing cities, established industries, and a population ready to shape its future. Logging, fishing, farming, and mining were still central to the economy, but new factories and businesses appeared in the Puget Sound region and beyond. With industrial growth came changes in how people worked and lived. Labor movements formed to demand better wages and safety, while social reformers fought for temperance, women's suffrage, and other causes. This chapter explores these early 1900s changes, showing how workers, reformers, and civic leaders reshaped Washington's society—paving the way for new ideas and regulations that would mark the era.

Rise of Labor Movements

Working Conditions at the Turn of the Century

As Washington's industries expanded, so did the workforce. Logging camps were larger, mills operated around the clock, and fishing canneries employed hundreds during peak seasons. Conditions remained tough: loggers faced falling trees and hazardous equipment, cannery workers handled sharp knives and hot steam, and miners continued to deal with cave-ins or toxic gases. Wages were often meager, and hours could stretch long, with few breaks.

City factories had their own challenges. Some produced lumber products, furniture, or processed agricultural goods. In these crowded workrooms, machines roared loudly, sometimes causing hearing loss or injuries if workers got too close. Since there were few government safety rules, each company set its own policies—usually aimed at maximum production rather than employee well-being. Over time, a sense grew among workers that they should unite to improve their circumstances.

Early Labor Unions

By the early 1900s, workers across Washington began forming or joining labor unions—organizations that negotiated on behalf of employees. The Knights of Labor, active nationwide, had chapters in certain towns. The American Federation of Labor (AFL) included smaller craft unions for carpenters, printers, and other trades. Miners joined groups that represented coal or hard-rock mining regions.

Union meetings took place in rented halls or back rooms of taverns, sometimes in secret if employers opposed union activity. Members discussed demands such as an eight-hour workday, safer conditions, and fair pay for overtime. They wrote leaflets and articles explaining their goals. Some unions organized strikes—work stoppages—if talks with company bosses failed. Strikes were risky: owners could fire the strikers, hire replacements, or even call in private guards to break picket lines. Still, union members believed that standing together gave them a stronger voice.

Major Strikes and Their Impact

Seattle Shipyard Strike (Early 1900s)

One notable labor action involved workers in the Seattle shipyards, where ships were built or repaired for transport and trade. As shipbuilding ramped up, owners demanded higher output with minimal pay increases. Skilled craftsmen—like boilermakers and riveters—complained of long hours and unsafe scaffolding. Fed up, they walked off the job, calling for better wages and a shorter workday.

The strike lasted several weeks, disrupting shipping schedules. Newspapers labeled the strikers as troublemakers, while union supporters rallied with marches downtown. Eventually, a compromise was reached: a modest pay raise and slight improvements in working conditions. Though not a complete victory, the strike showed that unified workers could force employers to negotiate.

Lumber Mill Strikes in Grays Harbor and Tacoma

Across western Washington, lumber mills hummed with activity, processing the region's vast forests. In places like Grays Harbor and Tacoma, millworkers organized strikes to protest low pay and dangerous sawmill floors. Owners insisted that lumber prices were unpredictable and that profits were slim. Strikers pointed out that many sawmill owners lived in large houses and enjoyed modern conveniences while workers lived in cramped, drafty housing near the mills.

Some strikes ended quickly when owners agreed to partial demands. Others dragged on, with occasional clashes between picketers and hired security guards. Local churches and women's groups often supported the workers, bringing food to picket lines or caring for families during the strike. Over time, these actions helped raise public awareness of harsh working conditions. Citizens began to ask whether it was fair for business owners to prosper so greatly while workers risked their lives for minimal rewards.

Political and Social Reforms

Women's Suffrage Advancements

Women in Washington had long pushed for voting rights, as discussed in earlier chapters. By the early 1900s, their efforts gained momentum. Suffrage clubs collaborated with labor groups, arguing that women who worked in factories, canneries, or as teachers deserved a direct say in the laws that affected them. Church organizations added moral weight, suggesting that women's votes could promote social purity and reduce vice.

In 1910, Washington women finally secured the right to vote. Although this date is just outside the immediate focus of "early" 1900s, the suffrage movement's main battles took place during the early years of the century, laying the groundwork for the final victory. Once enfranchised, women joined political parties, voted in local and state elections, and influenced legislation on education, child welfare, and prohibition. This change signaled that the old norms were shifting, allowing for a broader range of voices in civic life.

Temperance and Prohibition Efforts

Alcohol-related problems—drunken brawls, lost wages, and domestic abuse—had worried reformers since territorial times. The Woman's Christian Temperance Union (WCTU) and other groups organized rallies, passed out literature, and lobbied government officials to restrict or ban liquor sales. They believed that stopping alcohol consumption would improve families, reduce crime, and raise moral standards.

Some towns passed local "dry" laws, closing saloons. Others required bars to shut down on Sundays. As the movement spread, counties and eventually the state considered broader prohibition measures. These laws angered brewery owners, saloon keepers, and regular patrons who argued that moderate drinking caused no harm and that businesses would suffer. The temperance debate divided communities, pitting reformers against those who saw alcohol as part of social life. Still, the momentum for temperance kept growing, influenced by both religious convictions and labor concerns that drunkenness undermined worker productivity.

Ethnic Communities and Labor Movements
Role of Immigrant Workers

Washington's early 1900s workforce included many immigrants: Italians, Greeks, Japanese, Filipinos, and others who arrived seeking jobs. In logging camps, canneries, and railroad construction sites, they performed the hardest tasks. Often, they were paid less than white American workers, placed in segregated bunkhouses, and sometimes excluded from union membership.

Still, immigrant labor fueled Washington's expansion. For example, Japanese workers played a major role in the salmon canneries and on railroad crews. Filipinos labored in agricultural fields. Italians worked in quarries and on urban construction projects. Because they often lacked strong legal protection, these immigrants faced discriminatory practices from employers and local officials. However, some joined labor protests, forging alliances with American-born workers who realized that dividing workers by ethnicity only helped the bosses keep wages low.

Struggles and Achievements

A few unions attempted to unite all workers, regardless of background. This was especially true of groups influenced by progressive or socialist ideas, which argued that laborers should unite around class rather than nationality. Some successes included improved conditions in a few canneries that employed diverse groups. But tensions remained, and disagreements over language or cultural customs could hinder collective action.

Over time, ethnic communities formed mutual aid societies—like Japanese associations, Filipino clubs, or Italian fraternal lodges—that provided social gatherings, small loans, and assistance for the sick. These societies eased the burden of discrimination and gave immigrants a measure of self-help. Their existence also showcased Washington's growing cultural diversity, even though broader acceptance was still a struggle.

Social Shifts and City Life

Urban Expansion

Cities like Seattle, Tacoma, and Spokane experienced rapid growth in the early 1900s. Skyscrapers by that era's standards—maybe six or seven stories tall—rose downtown, hosting banks, department stores, and offices. Electric streetcars replaced horse-drawn trolleys, making it easier for people to commute from residential neighborhoods to factories or shops. Pavement slowly covered dusty roads, and sidewalks improved foot traffic. Some families enjoyed running water and electric lights for the first time, a sign of modern progress.

This urbanization brought new social opportunities: theaters showed plays and vaudeville acts, dance halls hosted lively nights, and restaurants served dishes reflecting the city's immigrant mix. Department stores offered ready-made clothing, a novelty in a state where many had once sewn their garments at home. Yet the gap between rich and poor was visible. Wealthy businessmen lived in grand houses on the hills, while laborers crowded into small apartments or boarding houses near industrial zones.

Changing Gender Roles

As more women entered the workforce—some as typists in offices, others as salesclerks or teachers—ideas about gender roles began to shift. Single women found jobs in growing cities and lived in all-female boarding houses, forging independence from family farms. Married women still often stayed home, but the presence of labor-saving devices like gas stoves or washing machines (in the better-off households) slightly reduced daily drudgery. This freed some time for community involvement or social clubs.

Church groups and women's clubs championed "maternalist" reforms, believing that women's nurturing instincts could improve society. They pressed for playgrounds in poor neighborhoods, better sanitation, and public health measures. Critics argued that women should stick to home life, but the tide gradually turned as more saw the benefits of women's contributions to civic improvements.

Technology and Transportation Changes

Automobiles Appear

By the early 1900s, the first automobiles appeared on Washington's roads, though they were rare and expensive. They typically belonged to wealthy individuals or business owners who saw cars as a stylish novelty. Most roads were in poor shape, full of ruts and mud, so driving was tricky. Mechanics who could fix these new "horseless carriages" were scarce. Despite such hurdles, local papers marveled at the future of automobile travel. Even if mass car ownership was still years away, the appearance of a single automobile caused a stir in small towns, drawing curious crowds.

Rail Improvements and Steamboats

Railroads continued to expand, connecting outlying farms to larger markets. Passenger service improved, with some trains offering sleeping cars or dining services for travelers heading across the state or beyond. Small towns built ornate train stations to impress visitors and potential investors.

Steamboats remained vital on waterways such as the Columbia and Snake Rivers, delivering goods and people to points unreachable by rail. Canals and improved docks facilitated trade. For many remote communities, the steamboat whistle signaled the arrival of mail, news, and fresh produce. Though these vessels had been around for decades, their continued use in the early 1900s highlights Washington's reliance on both land and water routes for commerce.

Progressive-Era Politics

Emerging Progressive Leaders

The early 1900s coincided with what historians call the Progressive Era, a time when people demanded reforms in government, business, and society. Washington, like many states, had politicians and civic leaders who championed progressive causes—government transparency, regulation of big companies, public education, and the direct election of U.S. senators (which was not yet standard across the country).

Local progressives argued that wealthy timber barons and railroad magnates wielded too much power, leading to corruption or environmental damage. They called for regulations to protect forests, limit overfishing, and ensure fair railroad shipping rates for farmers. Some progressive leaders also pushed for improved public health, like clean water systems in cities, and mandatory schooling for children to reduce child labor.

Legislative Reforms

In Olympia, lawmakers debated bills shaped by progressive ideals. One measure set up railroad commissions to oversee freight prices. Another tackled workplace safety rules for factories and mills. A few measures tried to curb child labor in canneries or garment shops, mandating that children under certain ages attend school instead of work. However, passing such laws was not always easy. Big business interests had allies in government who resisted any regulation that might cut profits.

Nevertheless, some reforms succeeded. Towns and cities embraced public ownership of utilities like water or streetcars, aiming to prevent private monopolies from gouging customers. The push for a direct primary system gave voters more say in choosing political candidates, reducing the hold of party bosses. Even though progress was uneven, these reforms indicated a growing belief that government should actively protect the public's welfare.

Cultural Developments and Entertainment

Vaudeville and Early Movies

In the early 1900s, vaudeville theaters flourished in Washington's cities. Vaudeville shows included variety acts: comedians, dancers, magicians, and jugglers. Traveling performers moved from one theater circuit to another. Families attended matinees, while adults enjoyed evening shows with slightly more risqué humor. These performances offered a welcome escape from workaday routines.

Moving pictures—at first just short silent films—began to appear in dedicated theaters called "nickelodeons," where a nickel bought entry. Pianists or small orchestras accompanied these silent reels. As film technology improved, longer movies and storylines emerged, attracting bigger crowds. Newspapers reviewed the latest films, praising their novelty. By 1910, movie houses were a common sight in major towns, marking the start of Washington's love affair with cinema.

Community Bands and Civic Arts

Local bands were also popular, with brass instruments leading parades on holidays or playing concerts in city parks on summer evenings. Children learned music in schools, sometimes forming youth ensembles. Choral societies sang patriotic anthems or hymns at public gatherings. Towns showed civic pride by funding bandstands or performance halls, where amateurs and visiting professionals could entertain audiences hungry for culture.

In some places, literary clubs evolved into small arts councils, hosting art exhibits, poetry readings, or traveling museum collections. These events might feature paintings of Washington's majestic landscapes, bridging the region's natural beauty with a growing artistic spirit. While day-to-day life could be rough for many workers, these cultural outlets provided balance, reminding the public that there was more to life than labor disputes and factory whistles.

Challenges and Tensions

Strikes Turning Violent

While some labor actions ended peacefully, others escalated. Employers sometimes hired armed guards or persuaded local sheriffs to break up picket lines. In certain cases, strikers fought back, leading to injuries or even deaths. Newspapers tended to blame labor agitators for any unrest, though workers insisted they only defended their right to protest.

Such tensions fueled debates about free speech, property rights, and the government's role. Progressive newspapers argued that these violent incidents revealed the need for fair labor laws. Conservative voices warned that union-led unrest threatened business growth. These arguments shaped public opinion, prompting some to question the extremes of either side.

Marginalized Communities

African Americans and Native Americans saw limited benefits from reforms. Discrimination continued, and job options remained slim. While labor unions sometimes welcomed Black members, prejudice within union ranks persisted, making it hard for them to hold leadership positions. Native communities were largely excluded from this new industrial order, confined to reservations or forced to adapt to wage labor in distant regions. Their cultural traditions often clashed with the era's rapid modernization, leaving them further on the margins of mainstream society.

A Glimpse of Washington's Next Phase

The Seeds of Greater Changes

By the mid-1900s—beyond our immediate scope—Washington would transform again, influenced by events like World War I, the Great Depression, and the growth of major industries. But in the early 1900s, one can already see the outlines of that future. Labor movements, progressive reformers, and an increasingly diverse population were redefining the social and political landscape. Factories and new technologies hinted at an industrial century ahead.

For many, optimism ran high. With each new law protecting workers or each progressive politician elected, people believed they were building a fairer, safer society. At the same time, conflicts over race, class, and the environment showed that not everyone shared equally in this progress. The next decades would test whether Washington could handle rapid change without leaving too many behind.

Chapter Summary

In this chapter, we delved into the social and labor shifts that marked Washington's early 1900s. We saw how harsh working conditions drove workers to form unions and strike for better pay, safer workplaces, and reasonable hours. We also glimpsed the rise of progressive politics, with social reforms targeting liquor laws, child welfare, and corporate control. Women's suffrage advanced, and immigrant communities found ways to organize despite discrimination. City life offered new cultural outlets—vaudeville, silent films, and local bands—while automobiles and improved railways hinted at future transformations.

All these developments signaled a state in transition: from a raw resource-based frontier to a place where citizens demanded a voice in shaping industry, government, and society. Yet many challenges—racial bias, environmental concerns, and class tensions—remained unresolved. In the next chapter, we will focus on some of the famous figures and local heroes who guided and inspired Washington during these formative years. Their leadership and accomplishments will give deeper insight into the human stories behind the state's evolution.

CHAPTER 18

Famous Figures – Leaders, Visionaries, and Local Heroes

Throughout Washington's early history, certain individuals stood out for their leadership, ingenuity, and impact on local communities. Some guided political decisions, while others shaped the economy, culture, or social reforms. A few are still well-known today, while others made their mark in quieter ways, leaving behind legacies that affected how towns developed, how rights were won, or how industries were run. This chapter shines a light on several notable figures—politicians, entrepreneurs, social activists, and local heroes—who played pivotal roles in the state's growth from its territorial days into the early 1900s.

Politicians and State Builders

Elisha P. Ferry (Washington's First Governor)

When Washington achieved statehood in 1889, Elisha Peyre Ferry became its first governor. He had previously served as territorial governor, giving him a unique perspective on the transition from territory to state. Ferry was known for his calm demeanor and administrative skills. He worked to organize state institutions, support public education, and foster infrastructure projects like roads and county courthouses. Though not a fiery orator, he steadied Washington's government during its formative years, ensuring a smooth transfer of power and helping the state legislature tackle early issues such as land disputes and resource management.

John R. Rogers: A Progressive Voice

Another key political leader in the late 1800s and early 1900s was John Rankin Rogers, who served as governor from 1897 to 1901.

Rogers championed the interests of farmers and workers, reflecting the populist and progressive spirit of the time. He pushed for more equitable tax laws, advocated for public ownership of certain utilities, and supported expanded public education. Known for his motto, "I would make every workingman a capitalist, every capitalist a workingman," Rogers tried to bridge class divisions through policy. Though he faced opposition from powerful business leaders, he remained a beloved figure among rural communities, who saw in him a politician who understood their struggles.

Entrepreneurs and Industrial Pioneers

Henry Yesler: Sawing the Way in Seattle

In Seattle's early history, Henry Yesler made a name for himself by establishing the city's first steam-powered sawmill in the 1850s. At that time, Seattle was a tiny settlement on Puget Sound, but Yesler recognized the value of milling lumber for both local building needs and export. His mill provided jobs, and its famous "skid road"—a path used to drag logs to the mill—eventually lent its name to Seattle's historic neighborhood, "Skid Row." Although he became wealthy, Yesler also donated land for city development and stayed involved in civic affairs. Many credit his sawmill as a key spark that put Seattle on the path to becoming a major urban center.

James J. Hill: The Railroad Titan

While not a Washington resident, James J. Hill profoundly influenced the state's growth by building the Great Northern Railway, which connected the upper Midwest to Seattle in the 1890s. Hill believed in efficient, low-debt construction and promoted settlement along his rail lines, urging farmers to move to the fertile lands of eastern Washington. Known as the "Empire Builder," he took a personal interest in how towns sprang up near the tracks. Though some criticized his power, few could deny the positive impact of dependable rail service. Hill's efforts ensured that communities off the main Northern Pacific line had access to national markets, boosting Washington's wheat, lumber, and mining industries.

Social Reformers and Activists

Emma Smith DeVoe: Suffrage Leader

Emma Smith DeVoe was a driving force behind women's suffrage in Washington. Arriving from the Midwest, she brought organizational experience and a gift for public speaking. DeVoe held rallies, trained local activists, and lobbied legislators. She believed in polite persuasion rather than confrontational tactics, winning supporters among male politicians who found her approach agreeable. DeVoe's leadership proved crucial in the campaign leading up to the 1910 suffrage victory. After Washington women won the right to vote, she continued to champion national suffrage, sharing the lessons learned from her successful work in the state.

Billy Frank Jr. (Early Efforts as a Young Man)

Although Billy Frank Jr. is most famously associated with the landmark "Fish Wars" and legal battles in the mid- to late 20th century (beyond the immediate scope of our timeframe), his early life in the 1900s sets an important stage. Growing up in a Nisqually family, he witnessed firsthand the restrictions on tribal fishing rights promised by 19th-century treaties but largely ignored by state authorities. As a youth, Billy helped family members fish in traditional waters, often facing harassment from officials. This early experience sowed the seeds of his later activism. While his greatest achievements came decades after this book's main focus, his story illustrates how early 1900s conditions shaped the Native leaders who would eventually fight to uphold treaty rights.

Cultural Figures and Educators

May Arkwright Hutton: Mining Camp Cook to Influential Citizen

May Arkwright Hutton started life in humble circumstances as a cook in Idaho mining camps, not far from the Washington border. Bold and outspoken, she eventually moved to Spokane, where she invested in mines and built a fortune. Hutton used her wealth and influence to support women's suffrage, labor rights, and social welfare causes. Known for her fiery speeches and flamboyant style—she wore bright clothes and large hats—she drew attention to issues like fair wages and the moral right of women to vote. Through both her financial contributions and her forceful personality, Hutton left a deep impact on the Spokane region's civic affairs.

Edmond Meany: Historian and Professor

Edmond S. Meany was an educator at the University of Washington who also served as a state legislator. He became well-known for his devotion to preserving Washington's history. Meany wrote several books documenting the state's geography, Native cultures, and pioneer experiences, ensuring that future generations could learn about early life in the region. He also guided many students on field trips to Mount Rainier and other natural landmarks, advocating for the appreciation of the state's environment. Meany's passion influenced the creation of historical societies and shaped how Washingtonians viewed their past—celebrating both pioneer achievements and natural beauty.

Local Heroes and Unsung Figures

Frontier Doctors and Nurses

Not all influential figures were politicians or wealthy entrepreneurs. Frontier doctors and nurses often risked their lives traveling long distances to treat patients with limited medicine and supplies. Individuals like Dr. Mary L. Thompson in Seattle, Dr. Minnie C. Peterson in small towns, or various unnamed nurses in logging camps exemplified dedication. They battled epidemics, delivered babies, and sewed up injuries from sawmill accidents. Their skill and compassion saved countless lives, yet they rarely received widespread fame. Communities often revered them as local heroes, organizing benefits to buy them better medical equipment or simply praising them in local newspapers for heroic service.

Teachers in Remote One-Room Schools

Similarly, teachers who braved remote one-room schoolhouses shaped entire generations. Some taught frontier children basic reading, writing, arithmetic, and a sense of civic duty. They might trek miles on foot or horseback to reach their tiny school each day. Low pay and isolation tested their resolve, but many stayed out of a sense of mission, believing education was the key to a stronger future. Although overshadowed by bigger names, these teachers forged bonds that kept communities alive, instilling hope in families who otherwise had few opportunities. Their quiet heroism remains in the memories of students who carried those lessons into adulthood.

Native Leaders' Roles and Challenges

Chief Moses and the Columbia Basin

In the late 1800s and early 1900s, Chief Moses of the Sinkiuse-Columbia people navigated a complex world as settlers flooded into the Columbia Basin. Though older treaties had stripped tribes of land, Moses worked with government agents to secure a reservation for his people. He faced criticism from some tribal members who felt he conceded too much and from settlers who believed any reservation was too large. Despite such pressures, Chief Moses remained a respected figure, trying to balance tribal survival with the unstoppable tide of settlement. Although overshadowed by more famous leaders, his diplomatic efforts eased conflicts in central Washington, allowing some tribal members to remain near their ancestral homeland.

Yakama and Spokane Leaders

Other tribal figures quietly led their communities through a maze of restrictive policies, ensuring cultural traditions endured. Yakama headmen negotiated grazing rights for cattle, while Spokane leaders arranged for schools that taught both English and traditional knowledge. Often lacking formal government recognition, these leaders used personal influence, trade relationships, and family ties to keep tribal identities alive. Their efforts paved the way for later activists who would demand treaty rights and cultural respect. Though rarely mentioned in mainstream historical accounts, they stand as pillars of resilience.

Military and Law Enforcement Heroes

Frontier Lawmen

As Washington settled into statehood, some areas still lacked a strong police force. Frontier lawmen—sheriffs, marshals, and deputies—tried to keep order in boomtowns and rural counties. Men like Harry Draper in Spokane County or John Partridge in southwestern Washington chased cattle rustlers, confronted bank robbers, and settled violent disputes in logging camps. While they were not always saintly—some had checkered pasts or used heavy-handed methods—their presence deterred outlaws and helped citizens feel safer. Newspapers covered their exploits, painting them as folk heroes or, in some cases, vigilantes if they bent the law to achieve justice.

Soldiers at Forts

Though major Native-settler conflicts had ended by the early 1900s, a few U.S. Army forts still operated in Washington. Soldiers there enforced federal laws, helped during natural disasters, and occasionally guarded prisoners. They also participated in local parades, boosting morale in nearby towns. While not engaged in major wars at home, their training and discipline inspired respect. Veterans from earlier Indian Wars or the Spanish-American War sometimes lived at these forts, sharing tales with younger troops and reinforcing a tradition of service.

Cultural Legacy of These Figures

Building the Washington Identity

The combined work of governors, entrepreneurs, reformers, and local heroes shaped Washington's early identity. Citizens looked up to them as role models or cautionary tales—learning from successes and failures. Over time, local historical societies, newspapers, and schools recorded their stories, passing them on to new generations. Streets, public buildings, and parks were sometimes named in their honor, ensuring that even lesser-known achievements weren't forgotten.

These figures also molded how Washington interacted with the rest of the nation. Politicians like John R. Rogers supported progressive ideas that gained nationwide attention. Railroad magnates like James J. Hill tied the region's economy to distant markets. Suffrage leaders like Emma Smith DeVoe inspired other states to follow suit. By the early 1900s, Washington was no longer an isolated corner of the U.S. but a participant in broad cultural, political, and economic currents.

Lessons and Inspirations

While some of these individuals were wealthy or politically powerful, others were ordinary men and women driven by a desire to help their communities. Their stories remind us that the state's progress depended on a blend of vision, courage, and collaboration. Politicians needed the public's support to implement reforms; business pioneers relied on workers and neighbors to build and maintain infrastructure. Teachers, doctors, and tribal leaders—though not always celebrated—kept the social fabric intact with patient dedication.

The sense of community these figures fostered became part of Washington's cultural DNA, influencing how future generations approached challenges—whether in social justice, technology, or environmental stewardship. Even those who left no grand monuments behind left intangible gifts: the memory of kindness, perseverance, and hope in a rapidly changing world.

Continuation into Modern Times

While our focus remains on the historical period up to the early 1900s, many of these figures' influences carried forward. Laws shaped under governors like Elisha Ferry and John R. Rogers laid foundations for later policies. The spirit of Emma DeVoe's suffrage activism reemerged in subsequent civil rights movements. Entrepreneurs like Henry Yesler passed on a legacy of invention and risk-taking that paved the way for Seattle's later prominence in business and technology.

Conclusion and Looking Ahead

In this chapter, we have met politicians who steered Washington's entry into statehood, entrepreneurs who fueled economic expansion, social reformers who fought for voting rights and workplace improvements, and everyday heroes whose dedication saved lives or preserved traditions. Their combined efforts forged a society that was more organized, more inclusive (though still imperfect), and more prepared to face the 20th century's challenges.

As we move toward the final chapters of this book, we will explore the regional differences within Washington—how eastern and western parts of the state developed unique traits—and then reflect on the enduring lessons and legacies from these early periods. The famous figures we've seen here show that Washington's story is not just about mountains, forests, and rivers, but about people with vision, courage, and deep devotion to the land and to one another.

CHAPTER 19

Regional Differences – Eastern and Western Washington

Washington is often described as a land of contrasts, split by the Cascade Range into two distinct regions. Western Washington is known for its lush forests, damp climate, and maritime industries, while Eastern Washington features a drier landscape with rolling plains, vast farmland, and a reliance on irrigation. These differences go beyond geography and climate; they have shaped settlement patterns, economic activities, and cultural practices from the state's earliest days. In this chapter, we will explore how these two halves of Washington developed unique identities up to the early 1900s. We will look at how the presence or absence of rain, forests, rivers, and transportation routes influenced everything from architecture to community life, forging identities that sometimes cooperated and sometimes clashed.

The Great Divide: The Cascade Range

A Natural Barrier

The Cascade Mountains run north to south through the center of Washington, forming a rugged barrier between west and east. Early explorers like George Vancouver and fur traders recognized that these peaks made travel difficult, forcing long detours around or through dangerous mountain passes. Tectonic activity, glaciers, and volcanic forces created tall summits such as Mount Rainier, Mount Adams, and Mount Baker. These towering volcanoes, often snow-capped year-round, influenced weather patterns by trapping moisture from the Pacific Ocean on the western slopes, leaving the eastern side in a rain shadow.

Throughout the 1800s, building reliable roads or rail lines across the Cascades proved challenging. During harsh winters, snowfall could block passes for months, isolating communities. When railroads like the Northern Pacific and later the Great Northern bored tunnels through the mountains in the late 1800s, they connected east and west more directly. Still, the mountains remained a cultural and economic dividing line. Residents on each side developed distinct ways of living, shaped by climate and available resources.

Influence on Settlement

Western Washington's early settlers tended to cluster around Puget Sound and other coastal inlets, traveling by water for trade and supplies. Meanwhile, Eastern Washington settlers often arrived via overland routes—trails from Oregon or the Midwest—and spread out on the plains where the soil was fertile but rainfall was scarce. The Cascade Range, for a long time, limited direct trade between the two regions. Even after statehood in 1889, people found it easier to trade with neighbors across state lines than with communities on the opposite side of the Cascades. These patterns left a lasting mark on how each region perceived itself and its role in Washington's overall development.

Western Washington: Forests, Fjords, and Maritime Life

Abundant Rain and Thick Forests

Western Washington's climate is characterized by abundant rainfall, especially in winter. Coastal areas like the Olympic Peninsula and around Puget Sound can see drizzle or outright downpours for many months, creating temperate rainforests lush with moss and enormous cedar, fir, and hemlock. This environment supported the state's first major industry: logging. From the 1850s onward, vast stands of timber drew in lumber companies and ambitious entrepreneurs who built sawmills along the water. Their logs were easily floated to mills and shipped out on schooners or steamboats.

Because of these towering forests, Western Washington's architecture and infrastructure leaned heavily on local wood. Early homes, churches, and schools were framed with timber, and even sidewalks in some towns were laid with wooden planks. However, heavy rains meant constant maintenance of roads and buildings. Settlers coped with muddy streets, frequent floods, and the need for sturdy roofs. Yet the same rain nourished gardens, berry fields, and fruit orchards in coastal valleys, providing a steady local food supply.

Maritime Connections and Fishing

With Puget Sound, the Strait of Juan de Fuca, and numerous bays and inlets, Western Washington found its natural highways in water routes. Canoes and small boats gave way to schooners and steam-powered vessels that transported goods and people from town to town. Cities like Seattle and Tacoma grew around bustling harbors, where logs, fish, and other exports were loaded. Ferries operated between islands and the mainland, knitting together communities that would otherwise be isolated by rugged coastlines.

Fishing became a central part of life for many. Salmon, halibut, and shellfish thrived in these cold, nutrient-rich waters. Early canneries sprouted in places like Bellingham, Anacortes, and on the Olympic Peninsula, employing workers during the busy harvest seasons. They packed salmon into tins for shipment to distant markets, fueling local economies. Coastal tribes also continued their millennia-old traditions of fishing and clam-digging, though increasing industrial pressure on fish stocks and tension over fishing rights shaped their experiences. By the early 1900s, overfishing and habitat changes from logging threatened some fish runs, hinting that Western Washington's prosperity from marine resources was not without limits.

Urban Centers and Cultural Life

As Western Washington's population boomed—particularly around Seattle, Tacoma, and Everett—these cities became cultural hubs. Immigrants from Scandinavia, Ireland, Japan, and other regions arrived, finding work in mills, canneries, or on fishing boats. The constant arrival of goods by ship also meant new consumer products reached general stores, fueling urban growth. By the early 1900s, streetcars ran on city streets, theaters offered vaudeville or early movies, and department stores sold ready-made clothes.

Churches and social clubs thrived, reflecting the diverse population. Lutheran congregations served Scandinavian communities, while Catholic parishes welcomed Irish and Italian families. Japanese-language newspapers circulated in Seattle, addressing issues important to immigrant laborers. Meanwhile, suffrage and progressive movements found strong support in urban areas, as women activists and labor leaders organized rallies in city squares.

Western Washington's maritime identity lent it a sense of outward-looking energy, linking the region to global trade routes and ideas from across the seas.

Eastern Washington: Plains, Irrigation, and Agriculture

The Dry Side of the Mountains

East of the Cascades, rainfall drops dramatically, creating a semi-arid to arid climate in some areas. The terrain ranges from high plateaus around the Columbia Basin to rolling hills in the Palouse region, known for its distinctive silt-loam soils that formed from ancient dust storms. Without the frequent rains of the west, early settlers initially had to rely on dryland farming techniques or find prime spots near rivers like the Columbia, Snake, or Yakima. Though the land was fertile when watered, the shortage of precipitation limited growth until irrigation systems were developed.

Winters can be cold, with snow lingering in valleys, while summers bring scorching heat. Homesteaders soon realized that if they harnessed rivers or built small dams, they could turn desert-like expanses into productive fields. As a result, irrigation districts appeared in places like the Yakima Valley, ushering in new possibilities for fruit orchards, vineyards, and row crops. By the early 1900s, farmers were cultivating apples, hops, potatoes, and more, shipping them to markets far away. This agricultural bounty became a cornerstone of Eastern Washington's identity.

Wheat and the Palouse Region

While orchard farming dominated some valleys, wheat rose to prominence in the Palouse region, covering rolling hills around Pullman, Colfax, and beyond. The loess soil, blown in from ancient dust storms, proved ideal for wheat. As mechanized plows and harvesters appeared (pulled first by horses, later by tractors), farmers could work larger acreages. Wheat harvest times turned into community events, with neighbors helping neighbors. Some families grew wealthy exporting grain via rail lines that connected to the Columbia River or to ports in Western Washington.

Yet this prosperity came with environmental costs. Plowing up native grasses led to erosion on the steep hills. Rainfall patterns, though modest, sometimes caused gullies to form in fields. Farmers also faced bust cycles when wheat prices fell, linking them to global market fluctuations. Still, the Palouse brand of wheat, recognized for its quality, helped define Eastern Washington as a breadbasket region by the early 1900s, contrasting sharply with the timber-based economy of the west.

Small Towns and Community Culture

Unlike Western Washington's large ports, Eastern Washington towns often sprang up around railroad stops, irrigation canals, or river landings. Places like Spokane, Walla Walla, and Yakima became regional centers for commerce and trade, each with its own character. Spokane benefited from mining wealth in nearby Idaho and Canada, while Walla Walla's farmland produced wheat and fruit. Yakima grew into a fruit-packing hub, shipping apples and pears across the country.

Community life revolved around county fairs, grange meetings, and church socials. Many families lived on isolated homesteads, so events like harvest festivals or Fourth of July picnics provided welcome breaks. Women's clubs and local newspapers offered a sense of togetherness. In the dryness of summer, some towns worried about wildfires or dust storms, forging a spirit of cooperation in the face of nature's challenges. The farmland ethic also shaped political leanings, with populist and progressive ideas resonating among those who felt overshadowed by big-city interests in the west.

Cultural and Economic Contrasts

Logging vs. Farming

A broad stereotype emerged: Western Washington's economy revolved around logging, fishing, and maritime trade, while Eastern Washington focused on wheat, cattle, fruit orchards, and mining. Although there was some overlap—orchards grew in the west and small mills appeared in the east—these stereotypes held enough truth to shape how each side saw the other. Westerners viewed themselves as industrially advanced, turning forests into cities, while easterners took pride in feeding the nation and pioneering large-scale agriculture.

From an early standpoint, this divide carried into labor practices. Millworkers and dockworkers in the west often joined unions and engaged in strikes, while in the east, farm labor organization was slower to develop, partly because farming families did much of the work themselves. The concept of big "company towns" flourished near logging camps on the coast, whereas eastern farmland typically hosted smaller individual homesteads. These patterns fostered different attitudes toward labor rights, government intervention, and private enterprise.

Political Divergence

In the late 1800s and early 1900s, differences in economic interests led to political disagreements. Timber barons in the west favored policies that allowed them to secure cheap land, while eastern ranchers and farmers called for irrigation funding and protective tariffs on imported wheat. As Washington's legislature convened in Olympia, lawmakers representing each region often clashed over how to spend state funds or regulate resources.

Additionally, railroad routes sometimes bypassed eastern communities, leading to frustration about uneven development. In the west, people worried that fish runs were being damaged by logging silt, while eastern representatives cared more about building dams for irrigation, which could block salmon migration. These tensions did not always boil over, but they created a persistent undercurrent of rivalry, each side feeling that the other misunderstood their needs.

Transportation and Communication Links

Overcoming the Mountain Barrier

Before 1900, crossing the Cascades was a real adventure. Wagons struggled over mountain passes, and winter travel was nearly impossible. Even native trails used by tribes like the Yakama or Snoqualmie were perilous for heavily loaded carts. Steamboats and trains served each region well but rarely connected them. Only when railroad tunnels such as the Stampede Pass Tunnel (completed in 1888) and later improvements allowed more regular travel did east-west commerce increase significantly.

Stagecoaches and later automobile roads eventually bridged the divide. By the early 1900s, some highways were planned to connect Seattle or Tacoma with Yakima and Spokane. Progress was slow, with steep grades and hairpin turns. Construction crews toiled in short summers. Despite these difficulties, each new road linking east and west contributed to a sense of unity, allowing farmers to visit Seattle's markets or loggers to explore orchard lands. Over time, telegraph lines and telephone connections also helped unify the state, though the mountains still tested engineers' skills.

Shared Markets and Cooperation

As industrialization advanced, both regions recognized mutual benefits. Eastern farmers needed western ports to ship their wheat and fruit. Western mill owners needed eastern coal or orchard produce, plus markets to sell lumber for barns and houses. Cooperative ventures arose—grain storage facilities near coastal ports, canning factories that processed fruit shipped over the mountains, and rail lines offering special freight rates for wheat or lumber. These commercial ties offset some of the old suspicions, fostering partnerships that enriched both sides.

Still, the tension lingered. Some eastern communities grumbled that Seattle businesses set shipping prices too high. Western businesses complained about "grain barons" controlling wheat distribution. While these debates continued into the early 1900s, they spurred a broader awareness that Washington was an interconnected whole. Urban newspapers in Seattle and Spokane started covering each other's major events, bridging cultural gaps and encouraging more statewide thinking.

Social and Cultural Exchanges

Religious and Educational Networks

Religious denominations that spanned the state helped bridge the regional divide. Catholic dioceses, Methodist conferences, and Lutheran synods held gatherings that brought together pastors from both east and west. Similarly, teacher associations and state college extension programs united educators around the need for improved schools. Institutions like the University of Washington in Seattle drew students from farm families in the Palouse, forging friendships that crossed the Cascades. Meanwhile, local normal schools (teacher-training colleges) appeared in Ellensburg and Cheney, serving the eastern population but also maintaining ties to the western part of the state.

Over time, these networks fostered social ties that transcended geography. Clergy or teachers returned to their congregations or classrooms with stories of how the other side lived, dispelling stereotypes and planting seeds of curiosity. Sunday school materials traveled by mail, offering glimpses of shared moral teachings. County fairs occasionally hosted visitors from across the mountains, featuring produce or craft exhibitions that showcased the variety of Washington's landscapes. These cross-region connections might seem small on the surface, but they laid a foundation for a more unified state identity.

Chautauqua and Traveling Shows

The early 1900s Chautauqua movement—traveling shows of lectures, concerts, and educational programs—brought speakers to both sides of the Cascades. Audiences listened to orators discuss topics from farming innovations to the latest scientific discoveries. Vaudeville acts also toured widely, entertaining in mining camps, logging towns, and farming communities alike. These traveling shows sometimes commented on the differences between east and west in comedic skits, generating laughter about the "rainy side" and the "dry side," but also acknowledging the shared experiences of hard work and pioneer spirit.

In some ways, these amusements were the cultural glue that reminded Washingtonians they were part of a single tapestry. A traveling preacher or temperance advocate might start in Seattle, hold revivals in Yakima, then press on to Spokane. They encountered different terrain and livelihoods, but their core message or show adapted to local interests. Over time, the lines between east and west became less about isolation and more about healthy rivalry, each side proud of its specialties while acknowledging the state's overall achievements.

Environmental Considerations

Over-Logging vs. Over-Farming

Both regions faced ecological challenges by the early 1900s. Western Washington had logged vast tracts of old-growth forests with little reforestation. Clear-cut hillsides led to erosion and damaged salmon streams. Newspapers occasionally warned of a future "timber famine" if cutting continued at the same pace. In Eastern Washington, the plowing of the Palouse hills and heavy livestock grazing caused soil erosion and dust problems. Irrigation in drier areas changed river flows, impacting native fish populations.

Awareness of these issues grew gradually, leading to early conservation ideas. Some progressive lawmakers argued for setting aside certain forest areas as reserves, while agricultural specialists advised farmers to rotate crops or plant windbreaks. Though genuine environmental regulation remained minimal, the contrasts in landscape degradation united some reformers who saw that nature's bounty, whether fish or farmland, was not endless. This budding sense of stewardship hinted that if the state was to remain prosperous, both sides needed to care for their resources responsibly.

Water as a Shared Resource

Rivers like the Columbia and Snake originate in or flow through Eastern Washington, then meander toward the Pacific. Salmon returning upstream linked the fate of coastal fishing towns with farmland far inland. Dams built for irrigation or early hydropower impacted salmon migration, sparking conflict between fisheries and agriculture. Though large dam projects such as Grand Coulee or Bonneville belong to a slightly later era, early smaller dams already showed that water usage had broad consequences.

By the 1900s, local newspapers sometimes debated water rights: Should priority go to farmers for irrigation, or should streams remain open for salmon runs vital to coastal communities? Tribal leaders pointed out that treaties guaranteed fishing rights that required healthy rivers. This interplay of water needs became a microcosm of the regional divide—each side recognized water's value, yet found it hard to strike a balance. Over time, these tensions pushed the idea that East and West Washington needed each other's viewpoints to craft statewide solutions.

Identity and Stereotypes

"Wet-Siders" and "Dry-Siders"

As the region matured, playful stereotypes formed. Westerners might call Easterners "dry-siders," teasing them about lack of rainfall and wide-open spaces. Easterners retorted that "wet-siders" lived in a land of perpetual drizzle, crowding into noisy port cities. These nicknames reinforced friendly rivalry, though they sometimes carried undertones of real friction. Newspaper editorials occasionally scolded lawmakers for pandering to "Seattle interests" or ignoring farmland concerns.

However, in times of crisis—like severe winter storms in the Cascades or market crashes—Washingtonians from both sides often came together. Urban charities sent aid to drought-stricken farming communities, and orchard owners shipped fresh fruit to hungry dockworkers during strikes. This mutual help revealed that differences were overshadowed by a deeper sense of interdependence. Over time, the image of a "bipolar" state softened into acceptance that each region contributed vital pieces to the whole.

Cultural Cross-Pollination

Despite barriers, the early 1900s saw more movement of people, ideas, and goods across the Cascades than ever before. Families who visited the other side for business or pleasure returned with stories. Students from Eastern Washington might attend the University of Washington in Seattle, while Seattle lumber families invested in farmland or orchard ventures near Wenatchee. Letters and telegraph communications carried news from city to farm, farm to city. Over time, these interactions blurred strict lines. Writers, artists, and musicians drew inspiration from both the forested coasts and the sun-drenched fields. This cultural cross-pollination enriched the state's literature, music, and traditions, weaving Eastern and Western threads into a distinctive Washington tapestry.

The Early 1900s Balance

Cooperation Through Progress

By about 1910, rail lines, telegraphs, and new roads had made it easier for the two regions to cooperate on trade, education, and politics. Progressives in both east and west teamed up to pass laws on conservation, labor rights, and public utilities. Women's suffrage leaders traveled from city halls in the west to rural gatherings in the east, uniting the cause across geographical divides. Agricultural fairs invited west-coast fisherman or loggers to display their crafts, bridging the knowledge gap about each other's livelihoods.

Although the basic stereotypes of "wet" vs. "dry," "industrial" vs. "agricultural," persisted, many recognized that Washington's real strength lay in this diversity. The state's farmland fed not only its own population but also shipping lines in Seattle and Tacoma, enabling those ports to supply vessels with grain for international trade. In return, coastal mills turned timber into building materials for barns and houses on the plains. The synergy of east and west began to define Washington's identity as a place of contrasts that somehow fit together.

Road to the Future

As the 20th century advanced, new developments—like improved irrigation districts, hydroelectric dams, highways, and the eventual growth of aviation—further connected eastern and western communities. The differences did not vanish, but they evolved. People from Yakima or Spokane traveled more easily to Seattle for business or cultural events, while city dwellers visited orchard country or hiked in the Cascades. The old suspicion that each side only looked out for itself remained in some political arguments, yet a broader perspective took hold.

By the end of this early 1900s era, Washington had forged a dual identity. It was a single state, yet one with two hearts: one beating to the rhythm of tides and timber, the other pulsing with the cycle of planting and harvest. This duality gave the state resilience—if one sector faced a downturn, the other might carry the economy through. Culturally, it offered variety—from maritime traditions to frontier farming. Ultimately, the interplay between Eastern and Western Washington became one of the state's defining features, setting the stage for further developments in agriculture, industry, and community life.

Concluding Thoughts

In this chapter, we've seen how geography and climate played a central role in shaping the lives of Washington's settlers, from the coast-hugging loggers of the west to the wheat-harvesting farmers of the east. The Cascade Range stood as both a physical and symbolic boundary, but over time, roads, rails, and shared economic needs brought these two worlds into closer contact. Differences in rainfall, resources, and attitudes remained, and even fueled productive competition. Yet beneath those distinctions lay an underlying unity: every part of Washington contributed to the state's broader success, relying on each other's strengths to grow and prosper.

As we move to the final chapter, we will reflect on the overarching lessons and legacies of this period, tracing how Washington's earliest foundations—in land, people, and institutions—continue to echo through its history. We will see that the story of regional contrasts is just one strand in a tapestry woven from many threads: Native heritage, immigrant influences, labor struggles, resource management, and evolving cultural norms. These elements collectively shaped a state that, while diverse, found ways to come together under a shared banner of hope and enterprise.

CHAPTER 20

Last Reflections on Early Washington – Lessons and Legacies

Our journey through the early history of Washington has taken us from the land's ancient geological formations to the coming of Native Peoples, from European exploration to missionary encounters, from fur-trade posts and early settlement to the forging of a territory and eventually a state. We explored conflicts, treaties, economic booms and busts, the rise of labor movements, cultural growth, and regional differences. Now, we stand at the final chapter, looking back on the legacies these centuries of change have left behind.

In these last reflections, we will review the key themes and lessons that have emerged. We will see how the state's diverse geography molded its economy, how Native communities faced monumental upheavals yet preserved core elements of their heritage, how settlers overcame daunting challenges to build communities, and how the interplay of cultures and industries set Washington on a path toward a dynamic, if sometimes tumultuous, future. This chapter will serve as a closing meditation on what early Washington's history can teach us about resilience, cooperation, conflict, and the power of collective identity.

Land and Nature: Foundation of Everything

The Power of Geography

Washington's story begins with its landscape. Millions of years ago, tectonic shifts, volcanoes, glaciers, and floods carved out mountains, valleys, and coastal waters. These physical features directed human settlement patterns, shaping which areas were easy to farm, log, or navigate by boat. Mountain passes determined trade routes, while rivers became crucial highways for Native communities long before roads existed. Understanding the land's form and climate is vital to comprehending the early conflicts over resources and the economic strategies that settlers adopted.

Native peoples understood these forces intimately. Their seasonal movements followed salmon runs, root harvests, and game migrations. Later, missionaries and fur traders relied on the same waterways, while farmers sought the most fertile soils and adequate rainfall. As we saw, Western Washington's wet forests and Eastern Washington's drier plains developed distinct industries—logging on one side, wheat and orchards on the other. Every chapter of Washington's early history rests on the bedrock of its geography, reminding us that no human endeavor occurs in a vacuum. The land both guides and limits our choices.

Environmental Consequences

From the earliest logging booms to intensive farming, people extracted resources at a rapid pace, often without long-term planning. By the early 1900s, eroded hillsides, depleted fish stocks, and decimated forests signaled that nature's bounty could be exhausted if not managed wisely. While robust conservation measures were slow to appear, the seeds of environmental awareness began to sprout. Leaders who recognized the perils of overcutting or overfishing laid groundwork for later policies. Even though formal environmental regulation was minimal in the early years, the experiences of resource depletion taught an enduring lesson: wise stewardship is essential for sustainability.

Native Peoples and Cultural Resilience

Continuity Amid Displacement

Washington's first inhabitants were tribes with rich traditions, extensive trade networks, and deep respect for the land. As settlers arrived, treaties were signed—often under duress—that ceded vast areas of tribal territory to the federal government. Conflicts like the Cayuse War, the Yakama War, and the Puget Sound War revealed the Native struggle against encroachment. Despite disease outbreaks, broken treaty promises, and forced relocation to reservations, many tribes maintained cultural continuity. Oral traditions, ceremonies, language instruction within families, and spiritual beliefs endured, even if practiced in secrecy.

This resilience underscores a vital lesson: even when faced with overwhelming external pressure, cultural identity can persist and adapt. Tribal leaders found ways to negotiate, sometimes forging uneasy alliances or adopting new agricultural methods to survive on restricted lands. Their determination inspired future generations who would later demand treaty rights recognition and cultural respect. For modern readers of this history, it is a reminder that behind every statistic of displacement is a community striving to sustain its language, family ties, and worldview.

Echoes in Legal Battles

The treaties from the mid-1800s—like Medicine Creek and Walla Walla—remained on the books. Though seldom honored in the immediate decades, they later became crucial legal documents for Native rights. Indeed, the early 1900s set the stage for future court cases over fishing, hunting, and resource sharing. Tribes argued that these treaties contained promises that never expired. While those battles mostly took place beyond the scope of this book, the seeds of those conflicts were planted in the years we covered, confirming that the earliest periods have direct bearing on modern legal and ethical debates about sovereignty and land use.

Settlement and Statehood

Pioneer Hardships and Community Spirit

From the moment the first wagon trains rolled west, settlers faced immense trials—diseases, harsh weather, difficult terrain, and sometimes hostile interactions with Native Peoples. Missions and fur-trade posts offered initial footholds, but large-scale settlement accelerated after the Oregon Trail migration. The creation of Washington Territory in 1853 brought a semblance of governance, yet constant challenges remained: building roads, organizing schools, establishing law enforcement. Despite meager resources, communities united around tasks like raising barns, planting crops, and forming social clubs or churches.

This pioneer spirit of cooperation left a cultural imprint that persisted into the statehood era. Collective efforts to found towns, help neighbors in distress, or hold community celebrations showed how mutual aid could mitigate frontier isolation. Such grassroots initiative laid the base for the progressive reforms of the early 1900s, revealing that the ethos of "neighbors helping neighbors" could evolve into more formal structures like labor unions, women's clubs, or civic associations seeking larger societal improvements.

Transition to a Modern State

Achieving statehood in 1889 signaled that Washington was mature enough for full membership in the Union. Governors like Elisha P. Ferry and John R. Rogers guided the young state, overseeing economic booms in logging, mining, and agriculture. Railroads connected distant corners, and legislative sessions tackled issues from resource management to tax structures. The expansion of schools, formation of counties, and enactment of state-level laws shaped everyday life. By the early 1900s, Washington boasted thriving cities—Seattle, Tacoma, Spokane—alongside rural farmland communities, each with its own identity but bound by a single state government.

Yet, statehood did not erase all tensions. Native treaty rights remained unfulfilled, labor disputes sometimes turned violent, and environmental depletion raised alarms. Still, the step from territory to state formed a common bond among residents who believed in Washington's potential to blend resource wealth with social progress. A sense of pride in the "Evergreen State" took hold, balancing a frontier legacy with modern aspirations.

Economic Ups and Downs

Fur Trade to Timber and Agriculture

Our chapters followed the shift from the early fur-trade economy—dominated by companies like Hudson's Bay—to a more diverse set of industries: logging in the western forests, fishing along coastlines, and farming in eastern fields. This evolution was driven by new technologies (like steam-powered saws) and by market demands (California's need for lumber, the global appetite for wheat). Each shift brought fortunes to some and disappointment to others.

Boom and bust cycles rattled families who staked everything on a single resource. Mining towns rose and fell, farmland markets soared then crashed, canneries thrived or closed depending on fish runs. Over time, some stability emerged through diversification and improvements in transportation. By 1900, the state's economy was no longer reliant on one staple. Logging, though still important, shared the stage with orchard harvests, wheat exports, and emerging industrial ventures. This varied economic base underpinned a more resilient state, able to weather periodic downturns better than monolithic economies might.

Labor Movements and Progressive Reforms

As industries grew, laborers demanded fair wages and safe working conditions, fueling strikes and union activities. Sawmills in Grays

Harbor, shipyards in Seattle, and mining operations in northeastern Washington all experienced labor unrest. The pushback from employers sometimes triggered violent clashes. Still, these struggles led to incremental reforms—shorter workdays, modest wage increases, and awareness that unbridled corporate power could harm the public interest.

The Progressive Era, which swept the nation in the early 1900s, found fertile ground in Washington. Lawmakers passed measures regulating railroad rates, improving factory safety, and banning child labor. Women's suffrage emerged victorious in 1910, capping decades of advocacy. Though not all groups benefited equally—immigrants, African Americans, and tribes still faced discrimination—these reforms planted the notion that government could be an engine for social good, not merely a distant authority. The interplay of economic booms, labor activism, and progressive ideals shaped a distinctive spirit in Washington's public life.

Cultural Growth and Integration

Churches, Newspapers, and Education

The territory's rough edges gradually smoothed as churches, newspapers, and schools knitted communities together. Congregations offered spiritual guidance, moral standards, and social gatherings that built unity. Newspapers, from small-town weeklies to city dailies, spread information on politics, labor issues, and local gossip. One-room schoolhouses laid foundations for literacy and civic engagement, while normal schools and the University of Washington trained teachers and future leaders.

These cultural institutions fostered a sense of belonging that transcended geography. A teacher from eastern farmland might move to a western logging town, bridging differences in local traditions. Newspaper editors visited Olympia or Seattle to gather news, distributing the same stories in smaller towns. Despite linguistic and cultural barriers among immigrant groups, a shared emphasis on reading, worship, and communal improvement helped unify people around basic civic values.

Social Clubs and Ethnic Communities

Women's clubs, temperance organizations, ethnic fraternities, and labor unions offered places where individuals found support and camaraderie. Ethnic enclaves—like the Scandinavian communities around Puget Sound or the Italian and Japanese ones in certain neighborhoods—maintained cultural traditions with local festivals, while also engaging in the broader American experience. Over time, some cultural boundaries softened as younger generations embraced English and participated in statewide activities such as county fairs or statewide suffrage rallies.

Nevertheless, prejudice lingered. Chinese Exclusion laws, anti-Japanese sentiment, and restricted job opportunities for African Americans proved that acceptance was uneven. Nativist attitudes sometimes flared in economic downturns, scapegoating immigrants. Yet, Washington's overall trajectory leaned toward gradual acceptance, with each wave of settlement adding unique threads to the state's social fabric. These layered identities gave Washington a complex cultural mosaic, a strength that would later manifest in distinctive arts, cuisine, and civic life.

Regional Differences: East and West

Complementary Economies

Chapter 19 explored how the Cascade Range split the state into contrasting zones—wet, forested west vs. dry, rolling east. Though this divide sometimes fostered rivalry, each side's economy complemented the other. Timber barons needed agricultural products and raw materials from the east; wheat farmers and orchardists needed the ports and mills of the west. Over time, railroads and roads lessened the isolation, forging trade networks that benefited both sides. Despite continuing stereotypes—"wet-siders" vs. "dry-siders"—cooperation gradually increased, especially as the state legislature tackled statewide concerns like resource management and infrastructure.

Cultural Interchange

Despite distinct regional identities, Washingtonians mingled through traveling shows, church conferences, and educational exchanges. Students from farmland counties attended colleges in coastal cities, while job-seekers from Seattle or Tacoma ventured east for orchard or ranch opportunities. By the early 1900s, letters, newspapers, and occasionally telephone calls (in wealthier districts) connected these contrasting lands. The tension between "industrial west" and "agricultural east" never fully disappeared, but it mellowed into a stable dynamic, each region proud of its heritage yet reliant on the other for statewide prosperity.

Lessons for Future Generations

Resilience, Cooperation, and Adaptation

The story of early Washington exemplifies how resilience and cooperation can transform a frontier into a functioning society. Native Peoples adjusted to upheavals by preserving core cultural elements. Settlers overcame harsh climates and isolation through community initiatives. Laborers fought exploitation with collective organizing. Even the state's geography, once a near-insurmountable barrier, was gradually bridged by innovative engineering. Each phase required adaptation—whether learning to plant wheat in arid soils, finding new markets for timber, or forging alliances among diverse ethnic communities.

The common thread is that no single group achieved success alone. From barn-raisings and road-building to progressive legislation, Washington's development depended on alliances and shared effort. This principle echoes in modern policymaking and community engagement, reminding us that the best solutions often arise from collaboration rather than competition.

The Challenge of Inclusivity

Washington's early history also teaches how difficult it is to achieve inclusivity. Many groups—Native tribes, immigrants, racial minorities, women—had to fight for recognition and rights. Some overcame barriers through determined activism, like the suffragists who secured the vote. Others, such as certain Native communities or ethnic groups facing restrictive laws, encountered partial or delayed justice. The tension between progressive ideals and discriminatory practices is an enduring lesson: societies can proclaim fairness while maintaining exclusions. Recognizing and addressing these contradictions is key to genuine progress.

Ongoing Legacy

Influence on Modern Washington

Even though this book focuses on early times, the legacies of that era ripple forward. Place names—Seattle, Tacoma, Spokane—still reflect tribal or pioneer influences. Logging, fishing, and agriculture remain significant industries, though modern regulations and technologies have changed their scale. Debates over water rights, salmon protection, and land use trace back to 19th-century treaties and resource extraction patterns. Progressive-era labor reforms paved the way for continued worker protections, while women's suffrage victory set a precedent for future civil rights expansions.

Culturally, the state's inclination toward open-mindedness and experimentation can be traced to diverse immigrant influences, early acceptance of new ideas in the Progressive Era, and the frontier spirit of forging solutions in a challenging environment. Artistic traditions reflecting both indigenous heritage and settler creativity have enriched Washington's identity. Even current political discussions about balancing economic growth with environmental stewardship echo the themes present in these early decades.

Preserving the Past

Historical societies, museums, and educational programs across Washington strive to keep early history alive. They preserve artifacts—from pioneer wagons to tribal artwork—and restore historic buildings where treaties were signed or rail deals were made. Public memorials honor figures like Chief Leschi, John R. Rogers, and Emma Smith DeVoe, while interpretive centers tell visitors about logging, mining, or orchard agriculture. These efforts remind us that knowledge of our roots fosters a deeper appreciation for the land, the people, and the struggles that shaped the state.

Meanwhile, tribal cultural centers highlight indigenous perspectives, offering language classes and exhibits that tell the stories from a Native viewpoint. Partnerships between tribes and local governments can lead to rethinking how historical markers are presented, ensuring that the narrative includes all voices. In essence, preserving the past is not just about nostalgia; it's about understanding the forces that continue to influence Washington's identity and future.

Closing Reflections

A Tapestry of Many Threads

If there is a single lesson to draw from Washington's early history, it is that the state represents a tapestry of many threads—geographic, cultural, economic, and political. No single group or factor can claim full credit for its development. Instead, each wave of newcomers, each industry, each legislative act, and each tribal negotiation contributed to the patchwork. Conflicts arose, sometimes violently, yet over time a fragile unity formed, rooted in mutual needs and a shared sense of place.

From the glacial valleys of the Olympic Peninsula to the rolling hills of the Palouse, from the deep basalt canyons of the Columbia to the high peaks of the Cascades, Washington's natural beauty also played a silent but influential role. It provided resources but demanded respect. Settlers learned to adapt their methods, shaping communities that could endure the region's climate extremes. Today's Washington, with its bustling seaports and expansive farmlands, cannot be fully appreciated without recalling this interplay of land and people.

Hope and Challenge

Throughout our chapters, two themes emerged repeatedly: hope and challenge. Early settlers hoped for prosperity, Native Peoples hoped to preserve their lifeways, laborers hoped for fairness, and progressive reformers hoped for a more just society. At the same time, these hopes ran into challenges—harsh terrain, epidemic diseases, exploitative companies, and systemic prejudice. The story of early Washington is one of striving to balance those hopes against obstacles. Sometimes solutions were found; at other times, the struggles carried forward to later generations.

But in that tension lies the essence of Washington's legacy: a place where determination, resourcefulness, and community spirit can overcome extraordinary odds, yet never without lessons learned along the way. The state's capacity to adapt and innovate, while honoring the cultural and natural heritage that shaped it, stands as a testament to the endurance of its people—past, present, and future.

Final Note

As we conclude this book, we remember that history is never a closed book. The early chapters of Washington's story continue to influence modern events—from tribal sovereignty cases to environmental regulations, from ongoing debates over labor rights to the distinct identities of eastern and western communities. Studying this formative era offers a roadmap of mistakes to avoid and successes to build upon.

By understanding how early Washingtonians navigated challenges, we find inspiration for today's complex world, where balancing economic development, cultural inclusivity, and environmental care remains a pressing concern. The lessons of cooperation, resilience, respect for diversity, and prudent resource management echo as powerfully now as they did when the first missions were built, the first treaties were signed, or the first fruit orchards blossomed. May these reflections guide future generations to cherish the land, respect all communities, and strive for a fair and vibrant society—just as the early inhabitants of Washington, in their own ways, endeavored to do.

Help Us Share Your Thoughts!

Dear reader,

Thank you for spending your time with this book. We hope it brought you enjoyment and a few new ideas to think about. If there was anything that didn't work for you, or if you have suggestions on how we can improve, please let us know at **kontakt@skriuwer.com**. Your feedback means a lot to us and helps us make our books even better.

If you enjoyed this book, we would be very grateful if you left a review on the site where you purchased it. Your review not only helps other readers find our books, but also encourages us to keep creating more stories and materials that you'll love.

By choosing Skriuwer, you're also supporting **Frisian**—a minority language mainly spoken in the northern Netherlands. Although **Frisian** has a rich history, the number of speakers is shrinking, and it's at risk of dying out. Your purchase helps fund resources to preserve and promote this language, such as educational programs and learning tools. If you'd like to learn more about Frisian or even start learning it yourself, please visit **www.learnfrisian.com**.

Thank you for being part of our community. We look forward to sharing more books with you in the future.

Warm regards,
The Skriuwer Team

www.ingramcontent.com/pod-product-compliance
Lightning Source LLC
LaVergne TN
LVHW012039070526
838202LV00056B/5543